THE 48 LAWS OF POWER

ROBERT GREENE, the author, has a degree in classical
studies and has been an editor at *Esquire* and other magazines.
He is also a playwright and lives in Los Angeles.

JOOST ELFFERS is the producer of *The 48 Laws of Power*
and also of

The Secret Language of Birthdays
with Gary Goldschneider

The Secret Language of Relationships
with Gary Goldschneider

Play with Your Food
with Saxton Freymann

THE 48 LAWS OF
POWER
CONCISE EDITION

ROBERT GREENE

A JOOST ELFFERS BOOK

P
PROFILE BOOKS

This concise edition published in Great Britain in 2002 by
Profile Books Ltd
3A Exmouth House
Pine Street
Exmouth Market
London EC1R 0JH

Derived from *The 48 Laws of Power*, which was first published in Great Britain
in 1998 by Profile Books and was first published in the United States in 1998 by
Viking, a division of Penguin Putnam Inc.

A portion of this work first appeared in *The Utne Reader*

Typeset in Baskerville by MacGuru Ltd
info@macguru.org.uk
Printed and bound in India by
Manipal Technologies Limited, Manipal

The moral right of the author has been asserted.

A CIP catalogue record for this book is available from the British Library.

ISBN-10: 1 86197 404 3
ISBN-13: 978 1 86197 404 4

CONTENTS

PREFACE

The feeling of having no power over people and events is generally unbearable to us – when we feel helpless we feel miserable. No one wants less power; everyone wants more. In the world today, however, it is dangerous to seem too power hungry, to be overt with your power moves. We have to seem fair and decent. So we need to be subtle – congenial yet cunning, democratic yet devious.

This game of constant duplicity most resembles the power dynamic that existed in the scheming world of the old aristocratic court. Throughout history, a court has always formed itself around the person in power – king, queen, emperor, leader. The courtiers who filled this court were in an especially delicate position: They had to serve their masters, but if they seemed to fawn, if they curried favor too obviously, the other courtiers around them would notice and would act against them. Attempts to win the master's favor, then, had to be subtle. And even skilled courtiers capable of such subtlety still had to protect themselves from their fellow courtiers, who at all moments were scheming to push them aside.

Meanwhile the court was supposed to represent the height of civilization and refinement. Violent or overt power moves were frowned upon; courtiers would work silently and secretly against any among them who used force. This was the courtier's dilemma: While appearing the very paragon of elegance, they had to outwit and thwart their own opponents in the subtlest of ways. The successful courtier learned over time to make all of his moves indirect; if he stabbed an opponent in the back, it was with a velvet glove on his hand and the sweetest of smiles on his face. Instead of using coercion or outright treachery, the perfect courtier got his way through seduction, charm, deception, and subtle strategy, always planning several moves ahead. Life in the court was a neverending game that required constant vigilance and tactical thinking. It was civilized war.

Today we face a peculiarly similar paradox to that of the courtier: Everything must appear civilized, decent, democratic, and fair. But if we play by those rules too strictly, if we take them too literally, we are crushed by those around us who are not so foolish. As the great Renaissance diplomat and courtier Niccolò Machiavelli wrote, "Any man who tries to be good all the time is bound to come to ruin among the great number who are not good."

The court imagined itself the pinnacle of refinement, but underneath its glittering surface a cauldron of dark emotions – greed, envy, lust, hatred – boiled and simmered. Our world today similarly imagines itself the pinnacle of fairness, yet the same ugly emotions still stir within us, as they have forever. The game is the same. Outwardly, you must seem to respect the niceties, but inwardly, unless you are a fool, you learn quickly to be prudent, and to do as Napoleon advised: Place your iron hand inside a velvet glove. If, like the courtier of times gone by, you can master the arts of indirection, learning to seduce, charm, deceive, and subtly outmaneuver your opponents, you will attain the heights of power. You will be able to make people bend to your will without their realizing what you have done. And if they do not realize what you have done, they will neither resent nor resist you.

Consider *The 48 Laws of Power* a kind of handbook on the arts of indirection. By studying the laws in this book, you will understand power and its properties. And by putting them into practice, you will be able to thrive in the modern world, appearing the paragon of decency while being the consummate manipulator.

LAW

1

NEVER OUTSHINE

THE MASTER

JUDGMENT

Always make those above you feel comfortably superior. In your desire to please and impress them, do not go too far in displaying your talents or you might accomplish the opposite – inspire fear and insecurity. Make your masters appear more brilliant than they are and you will attain the heights of power.

KEYS TO POWER

Everyone has insecurities. When you show yourself in the world and display your talents, you naturally stir up all kinds of resentment, envy, and other manifestations of insecurity. This is to be expected. You cannot spend your life worrying about the petty feelings of others. With those above you, however, you must take a different approach: When it comes to power, outshining the master is perhaps the worst mistake of all.

Do not fool yourself into thinking that life has changed much since the days of Louis XIV and the Medicis. Those who attain high standing in life are like kings and queens: They want to feel secure in their positions, and superior to those around them in intelligence, wit, and charm. It is a deadly but common misperception to believe that by displaying and vaunting your gifts and talents, you are winning the master's affection. He may feign appreciation, but at his first opportunity he will replace you with someone less intelligent, less attractive, less threatening.

This Law involves two rules that you must realize. First, you can inadvertently outshine a master simply by being yourself. There are masters who are more insecure than others, monstrously insecure; you may naturally outshine them by your charm and grace. If you cannot help being charming, you must learn to avoid such monsters of vanity, or find a way to mute your good qualities when in their company.

Second, never imagine that because the master loves you, you can do anything you want. Entire books could be written about favorites who fell out of favor by taking their status for granted, for daring to outshine.

Knowing the dangers of outshining your master, you can turn this Law to your advantage. First you must flatter and puff up your master. Overt flattery can be effective but has its limits; it is too direct and obvious, and looks bad to other courtiers. Discreet flattery is much more powerful. If you are more intelligent than your master, for example, seem the opposite: Make him appear more intelligent than you. Act naive. Make it seem that you need his expertise. Commit harmless mistakes that will not hurt you in the long run but will give you the chance to ask for his help. Masters adore such requests. A master who cannot bestow on you the gifts of his experience may direct rancor and ill will at you instead.

If your ideas are more creative than your master's, ascribe them to him, in as public a manner as possible. Make it clear that your advice is merely an echo of his advice.

If you are naturally more sociable and generous than your master, be careful not to be the cloud that blocks his radiance from others. He must appear as the sun around which everyone revolves, radiating power and brilliance, the center of attention.

In all of these cases it is not a weakness to disguise your strengths if in the end they lead to power. By letting others outshine you, you remain in control, instead of being a victim of their insecurity. This will all come in handy the day you decide to rise above your inferior status. If you can make your master shine even more in the eyes of others, then you are a godsend and you will be instantly promoted.

Image: The Stars in the Sky. There can only be one sun at a time. Never obscure the sunlight, or rival the sun's brilliance, but rather fade into the sky and find ways to heighten the master star's intensity.

Authority: Avoid outshining the master. All superiority is odious, but the superiority of a subject over his prince is not only stupid, it is fatal. This is a lesson that the stars in the sky teach us – they may be related to the sun, and just as brilliant, but they never appear in her company. (Baltasar Gracian, 1601–1658)

NEVER PUT TOO MUCH TRUST IN FRIENDS, LEARN HOW TO USE ENEMIES

JUDGMENT

Be wary of friends – they will betray you more quickly, for they are easily aroused to envy. They also become spoiled and tyrannical. But hire a former enemy and he will be more loyal than a friend, because he has more to prove. In fact you have more to fear from friends than from enemies. If you have no enemies, find a way to make them.

King Hiero
chanced upon a
time, speaking
with one of his
enemies, to be
told ... that he
had stinking
breath.
Whereupon the
good king, being
somewhat
dismayed in
himself, as soon
as he returned
home chided his
wife, "How does
it happen that
you never told
me of this
problem?" The
woman, being a
simple, chaste,
and harmless
dame, said, "Sir,
I had thought all
men's breath had
smelled so."
Thus it is plain
that faults that
are evident to the
senses, gross and
corporal, or
otherwise
notorious to the
world, we know
by our enemies
sooner than by
our friends and
familiars.

PLUTARCH,
c.46–120 A.D.

KEYS TO POWER

It is natural to want to employ your friends when you find yourself in times of need. The world is a harsh place, and your friends soften the harshness. Besides, you know them. Why depend on a stranger when you have a friend at hand?

The problem is that you often do not know your friends as well as you imagine. Friends often agree on things in order to avoid an argument. They cover up their unpleasant qualities so as to not offend each other. They laugh extra hard at each other's jokes. Since honesty rarely strengthens friendship, you may never know how a friend truly feels. Friends will say that they love your poetry, adore your music, envy your taste in clothes – maybe they mean it, often they do not.

When you decide to hire a friend, you gradually discover the qualities he or she has kept hidden. Strangely enough, it is your act of kindness that unbalances everything. People want to feel they deserve their good fortune. The receipt of a favor can become oppressive: It means you have been chosen because you are a friend, not necessarily because you are deserving. There is almost a touch of condescension in the act of hiring friends that secretly afflicts them.

The problem with using or hiring friends is that it will inevitably limit your power. The friend is rarely the one who is most able to help you; and in the end, skill and competence are far more important than friendly feelings.

All working situations require a kind of distance between people. You are trying to work, not make friends; friendliness (real or false) only obscures that fact. The key to power, then, is the ability to judge who is best able to further your interests in all situations.

Your enemies, on the other hand, are an untapped gold mine that you must learn to exploit. When Talleyrand, Napoleon's Foreign Minister, decided in 1807 that his boss was leading France to ruin, and the time had come to turn against him, he understood the dangers of conspiring against the emperor; he needed a partner, a confederate – what friend could he trust in such a project? He chose Fouché, head of the secret police, his most hated enemy, a man who had even tried to have him assassinated. He knew that their former hatred would create an opportunity for an emotional reconciliation. He knew that Fouché would expect nothing from him, and in fact would work to prove that he was worthy of Talleyrand's choice; a person who has something to prove will move mountains for you. Finally he knew that his relationship with Fouché would be based on mutual self-interest, and would not be contaminated by personal feeling. The selection proved perfect; although the conspirators did not succeed in toppling Napoleon, the union of such powerful but unlikely partners generated much interest in the cause; opposition to the Emperor slowly began to spread. And from then on, Talleyrand and Fouché had a fruitful working relationship. Whenever you can, bury the hatchet with an enemy, and make a point of putting him in your service.

Never let the presence of enemies upset

Men are more ready to repay an injury than a benefit, because gratitude is a burden and revenge a pleasure.

TACITUS,
C.55–120 A.D.

or distress you – you are far better off with a declared opponent or two than not knowing where your real enemies lie. The man of power welcomes conflict, using enemies to enhance his reputation as a sure-footed fighter who can be relied upon in times of uncertainty.

Image: The Jaws of Ingratitude. Knowing what would happen if you put a finger in the mouth of a lion, you would stay clear of it. With friends you will have no such caution, and if you hire them, they will eat you alive with ingratitude.

Authority: Know how to use enemies for your own profit. You must learn to grab a sword not by its blade, which would cut you, but by the handle, which allows you to defend yourself. The wise man profits more from his enemies than a fool from his friends. (Baltasar Gracian, 1601–1658)

CONCEAL YOUR

INTENTIONS

JUDGMENT

*Keep people off balance and in the dark by never reveal-
ing the purpose behind your actions. If they have no clue
what you are up to, they cannot prepare a defense. Guide
them far enough down the wrong path, envelop them in
enough smoke, and by the time they realize your intentions, it will be too late.*

KEYS TO POWER

Do not be held a cheat, even though it is impossible to live today without being one. Let your greatest cunning lie in covering up what looks like cunning.

BALTASAR
GRACIAN,
1601–1658

Most people are open books. They say what they feel, blurt out their opinions at every opportunity, and constantly reveal their plans and intentions. They do this for several reasons. First, it is easy and natural to always want to talk about one's feelings and plans for the future. It takes effort to control your tongue and monitor what you reveal. Second, many believe that by being honest and open they are winning people's hearts and showing their good nature. They are greatly deluded. Honesty is actually a blunt instrument, which bloodies more than it cuts. Your honesty is likely to offend people; it is much more prudent to tailor your words, telling people what they want to hear rather than the coarse and ugly truth of what you feel or think. More important, by being unabashedly open you make yourself so predictable and familiar that it is almost impossible to respect or fear you, and power will not accrue to a person who cannot inspire such emotions.

If you yearn for power, quickly lay honesty aside, and train yourself in the art of concealing your intentions. Master the art and you will always have the upper hand. Basic to an ability to conceal one's intentions is a simple truth about human nature: Our first instinct is to always trust appearances. We cannot go around doubting the reality of what we see and hear – constantly imagining that appearances concealed something else would exhaust and terrify us. This fact makes it relatively easy to conceal one's intentions. Simply dangle an object you seem to desire, a goal you seem to aim for, in front of people's eyes and they will take the appearance for reality.

One way to hide your intentions is to talk endlessly about your desires and goals – just not your real ones. You will kill three birds with one stone: You appear friendly, open, and trusting; you conceal your intentions; and you send your rivals on time-consuming wild-goose chases.

Another powerful tool in throwing people off the scent is false sincerity. People easily mistake sincerity for honesty. Seeming to believe what you say gives your words great weight. This is how Iago deceived and destroyed Othello: Given the depth of his emotions, the apparent sincerity of his concerns about Desdemona's supposed infidelity, how could Othello distrust him?

If you believe that deceivers are colorful folk who mislead with elaborate lies and tall tales, you are greatly mistaken. The best deceivers utilize a bland and inconspicuous front that calls no attention to themselves. They know that extravagant words and gestures immediately raise suspicion. Instead, they envelop their targets in the familiar, the banal, the harmless.

Once you have lulled people's attention with the familiar, they will not notice the deception being perpetrated behind their backs. The grayer and more uniform the smoke in your smokescreen, the better it conceals your intentions.

The simplest form of smokescreen is facial expression. Behind a bland, unreadable exterior, all sorts of mayhem can be planned, without detection. This is a weapon that the most powerful men in history have

SNEAK ACROSS THE OCEAN IN BROAD DAYLIGHT

This means to create a front that eventually becomes imbued with an atmosphere or impression of familiarity, within which the strategist may maneuver unseen while all eyes are trained to see obvious familiarities.

FROM "THE THIRTY SIX STRATEGIES," QUOTED IN THOMAS CLEARY, THE JAPANESE ART OF WAR, 1991

learned to perfect. It was said that no one could read Franklin D. Roosevelt's face. Baron James Rothschild made a lifelong practice of disguising his real thoughts behind bland smiles and nondescript looks.

Remember: It takes patience and humility to dull your brilliant colors, to put on the mask of the inconspicuous. Do not despair at having to wear such a bland mask – it is often your unreadability that draws people to you and makes you appear a person of power.

Image: A Sheep's Skin. A sheep never marauds, a sheep never deceives, a sheep is magnificently dumb and docile. With a sheep-skin on his back, a fox can pass right into the chicken coop.

Authority: Have you ever heard of a skillful general, who intends to surprise a citadel, announcing his plan to his enemy? Conceal your purpose and hide your progress; do not disclose the extent of your designs until they cannot be opposed, until the combat is over. Win the victory before you declare the war. In a word, imitate those warlike people whose designs are not known except by the ravaged country through which they have passed. (Ninon de l'Enclos, 1623–1706)

ALWAYS SAY LESS
THAN NECESSARY

JUDGMENT

When you are trying to impress people with words, the more you say, the more common you appear, and the less in control. Even if you're saying something banal, it will seem original if you make it vague, open-ended, and sphinxlike. Powerful people impress and intimidate by saying less. The more you say, the more likely you are to say something foolish.

Power is in many ways a game of appearances, and when you say less than necessary, you inevitably appear greater and more powerful than you are. Your silence will make other people uncomfortable. Humans are machines of interpretation and explanation; they have to know what you are thinking. When you carefully control what you reveal, they cannot pierce your intentions or your meaning.

Your short answers and silences will put them on the defensive, and they will jump in, nervously filling the silence with all kinds of comments that will reveal valuable information about them and their weaknesses. They will leave a meeting with you feeling as if they had been robbed, and they will go home and ponder your every word. This extra attention to your brief comments will only add to your power.

As a young man, the artist Andy Warhol had the revelation that it was generally impossible to get people to do what you wanted them to do by talking to them. They would turn against you, subvert your wishes, disobey you out of sheer perversity. He once told a friend, "I learned that you actually have more power when you shut up."

In his later life Warhol employed this strategy with great success. His interviews were exercises in oracular speech: He would say something vague and ambiguous, and the interviewer would twist in circles trying to figure it out, imagining there was something profound behind his often meaningless phrases. Warhol rarely talked about his work; he let others do the interpreting. The

Down on his luck, [the screenwriter] Michael Arlen went to New York in 1944. To drown his sorrows he paid a visit to the famous restaurant "21." In the lobby, he ran into Sam Goldwyn, who offered the somewhat impractical advice that he should buy racehorses. At the bar Arlen met Louis B. Mayer, an old acquaintance, who asked him what were his plans for the future. "I was just talking to Sam Goldwyn ..." began Arlen. "How much did he offer you?" interrupted Mayer. "Not enough," he replied evasively. "Would you take fifteen thousand for thirty weeks?" asked Mayer. No hesitation this

less he said about his work, the more people talked about it. And the more they talked, the more valuable his work became.

By saying less than necessary you create the appearance of meaning and power. Also, the less you say, the less risk you run of saying something foolish, even dangerous. In 1825, a new czar, Nicholas I, ascended the throne of Russia. A rebellion immediately broke out, led by liberals demanding that the country modernize – that its industries and civil structures catch up with the rest of Europe. Brutally crushing this rebellion (the Decembrist Uprising), Nicholas I sentenced one of its leaders, Kondraty Ryleyev, to death. On the day of the execution Ryleyev stood on the gallows, the noose around his neck. The trapdoor opened – but as Ryleyev dangled, the rope broke, dashing him to the ground. At the time, events like this were considered signs of providence or heavenly will, and a man saved from execution this way was usually pardoned. As Ryleyev got to his feet, bruised and dirtied but believing his neck had been saved, he called out to the crowd, "You see, in Russia they don't know how to do anything properly, not even how to make rope!"

A messenger immediately went to the Winter Palace with news of the failed hanging. Vexed by this disappointing turnabout, Nicholas I nevertheless began to sign the pardon. But then: "Did Ryleyev say anything after this miracle?" the czar asked the messenger. "Sire," the messenger replied, "he said that in Russia they don't even know how to make rope."

"In that case," said the Czar, "let us

time. "Yes," said Arlen.

FROM THE LITTLE, BROWN BOOK OF ANECDOTES, CLIFTON FADIMAN, ED.

prove the contrary," and he tore up the pardon. The next day Ryleyev was hanged again. This time the rope did not break.

Learn the lesson: Once the words are out, you cannot take them back. Keep them under control. Be particularly careful with sarcasm: The momentary satisfaction you gain with your biting words will be outweighed by the price you pay.

Image:
The Oracle at Delphi. When visitors consulted the Oracle, the priestess would utter a few enigmatic words that seemed full of meaning and import. No one disobeyed the words of the Oracle – they held power over life and death.

Authority: Never start moving your own lips and teeth before the subordinates do. The longer I keep quiet, the sooner others move their lips and teeth. As they move their lips and teeth, I can thereby understand their real intentions … If the sovereign is not mysterious, the ministers will find opportunity to take and take. (Han Fei Tzu, Chinese philosopher, third century B.C.)

SO MUCH DEPENDS ON REPUTATION – GUARD IT WITH YOUR LIFE

JUDGMENT

Reputation is the cornerstone of power. Through reputation alone you can intimidate and win; once it slips, however, you are vulnerable, and will be attacked on all sides. Make your reputation unassailable. Always be alert to potential attacks and thwart them before they happen. Meanwhile, learn to destroy your enemies by opening holes in their own reputations. Then stand aside and let public opinion hang them.

KEYS TO POWER

The people around us, even our closest friends, will always to some extent remain mysterious and unfathomable. Their characters have secret recesses that they never reveal. The unknowableness of other people could prove disturbing if we thought about it long enough, since it would make it impossible for us really to judge other people. So we prefer to ignore this fact, and to judge people on their appearances, on what is most visible to our eyes – clothes, gestures, words, actions. In the social realm, appearances are the barometer of almost all of our judgments, and you must never be misled into believing otherwise. One false slip, one awkward or sudden change in your appearance, can prove disastrous.

This is the reason for the supreme importance of making and maintaining a reputation that is of your own creation.

That reputation will protect you in the dangerous game of appearances, distracting the probing eyes of others from knowing what you are really like, and giving you a degree of control over how the world judges you – a powerful position to be in.

In the beginning, you must work to establish a reputation for one outstanding quality, whether generosity or honesty or cunning. This quality sets you apart and gets other people to talk about you. You then make your reputation known to as many people as possible (subtly, though; take care to build slowly, and with a firm foundation), and watch as it spreads like wildfire.

A solid reputation increases your presence and exaggerates your strengths without your having to spend much energy. It can also create an aura around you that will instill respect, even fear. In the fighting in the North African desert during World War II, the German general Erwin Rommel had a reputation for cunning and for deceptive maneuvering that struck terror into everyone who faced him. Even when his forces were depleted, and when British tanks outnumbered his by five to one, entire cities would be evacuated at the news of his approach.

Make your reputation simple and base it on one sterling quality. This single quality – efficiency, say, or seductiveness – becomes a kind of calling card that announces your presence and places others under a spell.

Reputation is a treasure to be carefully collected and hoarded. Especially when you are first establishing it, you must protect it strictly, anticipating all attacks on it. Once it is solid, do not let yourself get angry or defensive at the slanderous comments of your enemies – that reveals insecurity, not confidence in your reputation. Take the high road instead, and never appear desperate in your self-defense. On the other hand, an attack on another man's reputation is a potent weapon, particularly when you have less power than he does. He has much more to lose in such a battle, and your own thus-far-small reputation gives him a small target when he tries to return your fire. But this tactic must be practiced with skill; you must not seem to engage in petty vengeance. If you do not break your enemy's reputation cleverly, you will inadvertently ruin your own.

Never go too far in your attacks, for that will draw more attention to your own

It is easier to cope with a bad conscience than with a bad reputation.

FRIEDRICH NIETZSCHE, 1844–1900

vengefulness than to the person you are slandering. When your own reputation is solid, use subtler tactics, such as satire and ridicule, to weaken your opponent while making you out as a charming rogue. The mighty lion toys with the mouse that crosses his path – any other reaction would mar his fearsome reputation.

Image:
A Mine Full
of   Diamonds
and Rubies. You
dug for it, you found it,
and your wealth is now
assured. Guard it with your
life. Robbers and thieves will
appear from all sides. Never take
your wealth for granted, and constantly
renew it – time will diminish the jewels'
luster, and bury them from sight.

Authority: Therefore I should wish our courtier to bolster up his inherent worth with skill and cunning, and ensure that whenever he has to go where he is a stranger, he is preceded by a good reputation ... For the fame which appears to rest on the opinions of many fosters a certain unshakable belief in a man's worth which is then easily strengthened in minds already thus   disposed   and   prepared. (Baldassare Castiglione, 1478–1529)

LAW
6

COURT ATTENTION
AT ALL COSTS

JUDGMENT

Everything is judged by its appearance; what is unseen counts for nothing. Never let yourself get lost in the crowd, then, or buried in oblivion. Stand out. Be conspicuous, at all costs. Make yourself a magnet of attention by appearing larger, more colorful, more mysterious than the bland and timid masses.

*A wasp named
Pin Tail was
long in quest of
some deed that
would make him
forever famous.
So one day he
entered the
king's palace and
stung the little
prince, who was
in bed. The
prince awoke
with loud cries.
The king and his
courtiers rushed
in to see what
had happened.
The prince was
yelling as the
wasp stung him
again and again.
The courtiers
tried to catch the
wasp, and each
in turn was
stung. The whole
royal household
rushed in, the
news soon
spread, and
people flocked
to the palace.
The city was in
an uproar, all
business
suspended.-Said
the wasp to itself,
before it expired
from its efforts,
"A name without*

KEYS TO POWER

Burning more brightly than those around
you is a skill that no one is born with. You
have to learn to attract attention. At the start
of your career, you must attach your name
and reputation to a quality, an image, that
sets you apart from other people. This image
can be something like a characteristic style of
dress, or a personality quirk that amuses people and gets talked about. Once the image is
established, you have an appearance, a place
in the sky for your star.

It is a common mistake to imagine that
this peculiar appearance of yours should not
be controversial, that to be attacked is somehow bad. Nothing could be farther from the
truth. To avoid being a flash in the pan, and
having your notoriety eclipsed by another,
you must not discriminate between different
types of attention; in the end, every kind will
work in your favor.

The court of Louis XIV contained
many talented writers, artists, great beauties,
and men and women of impeccable virtue,
but no one was more talked about than the
singular Duc de Lauzun. The duke was short,
almost dwarfish, and he was prone to the
most insolent kinds of behavior – he slept
with the king's mistress, and openly insulted
not only other courtiers but the king himself.
Louis, however, was so beguiled by the
duke's eccentricities that he could not bear
his absences from the court. It was simple:
The strangeness of the duke's character
attracted attention. Once people were
enthralled by him, they wanted him around
at any cost.

Society craves larger-than-life figures,

people who stand above the general mediocrity. Never be afraid, then, of the qualities that set you apart and draw attention to you. Court controversy, even scandal. It is better to be attacked, even slandered, than ignored.

If you find yourself in a lowly position that offers little opportunity for you to draw attention, an effective trick is to attack the most visible, most famous, most powerful person you can find. When Pietro Aretino, a young Roman servant boy of the early sixteenth century, wanted to get attention as a writer of verses, he decided to publish a series of satirical poems ridiculing the pope and his affection for a pet elephant. The attack put Aretino in the public eye immediately. A slanderous attack on a person in a position of power would have a similar effect. Remember, however, to use such tactics sparingly after you have the public's attention, when the act can wear thin.

Once in the limelight you must constantly renew it by adapting and varying your method of courting attention. If you don't, the public will grow tired, will take you for granted, and will move on to a newer star. The game requires constant vigilance and creativity. Pablo Picasso never allowed himself to fade into the background; if his name became too attached to a particular style, he would deliberately upset the public with a new series of paintings that went against all expectations. Better to create something ugly and disturbing, he believed, than to let viewers grow too familiar with his work. Understand: People feel superior to the person whose actions they can predict. If you show them who is in control by playing

fame is like fire without flame. There is nothing like attracting notice at any cost."

INDIAN FABLE

Even when I'm
railed at, I get
my quota of
renown.

PIETRO ARETINO,
1492–1556

against their expectations, you both gain their respect and tighten your hold on their fleeting attention.

Image:
The Limelight. The
actor who steps into this
brilliant light attains a height-
ened presence. All eyes are on him.
There is room for only one actor at a
time in the limelight's narrow
beam; do whatever it takes to make
yourself its focus. Make your gestures so large, amusing, and scan-
dalous that the light stays on
you while the other actors
are left in the shadows.

Authority: Be ostentatious and be
seen … What is not seen is as though
it did not exist … It was light that
first caused all creation to shine
forth. Display fills up many blanks,
covers up deficiencies, and gives
everything a second life, especially
when it is backed by genuine merit.
(Baltasar Gracian, 1601–1658)

GET OTHERS TO DO THE WORK FOR YOU, BUT ALWAYS TAKE THE CREDIT

JUDGMENT

Use the wisdom, knowledge, and legwork of other people to further your own cause. Not only will such assistance save you valuable time and energy, it will give you a god-like aura of efficiency and speed. In the end your helpers will be forgotten and you will be remembered. Never do yourself what others can do for you.

A hen who had
lost her sight,
and was
accustomed to
scratching up the
earth in search
of food,
although blind,
still continued to
scratch away
most diligently.
Of what use was
it to the
industrious fool?
Another sharp-
sighted hen, who
spared her
tender feet, never
moved from her
side, and
enjoyed, without
scratching, the
fruit of the
other's labor. For
as often as the
blind hen
scratched up a
barley-corn, her
watchful
companion
devoured it.

FABLES,
GOTTHOLD
LESSING,
1729–1781

KEYS TO POWER

The world of power has the dynamics of the jungle: There are those who live by hunting and killing, and there are also vast numbers of creatures (hyenas, vultures) who live off the hunting of others. These latter, less imaginative types are often incapable of doing the work that is essential for the creation of power. They understand early on, though, that if they wait long enough, they can always find another animal to do the work for them. Do not be naive: At this very moment, while you are slaving away on some project, there are vultures circling above trying to figure out a way to survive and even thrive off your creativity. It is useless to complain about this, or to wear yourself ragged with bitterness. Better to protect yourself and join the game. Once you have established a power base, become a vulture yourself, and save yourself a lot of time and energy.

The artist Peter Paul Rubens, late in his career, found himself deluged with requests for paintings. He created a system: In his large studio he employed dozens of outstanding painters, one specializing in robes, another in backgrounds, and so on. He created a vast production line in which a large number of canvases would be worked on at the same time. When an important client visited the studio, Rubens would shoo his hired painters out for the day. While the client watched from a balcony, Rubens would work at an incredible pace, with unbelievable energy. The client would leave in awe of this prodigious man, who could paint so many masterpieces in so short a time.

This is the essence of the Law: Learn to get others to do the work for you while you take the credit, and you appear to be of godlike strength and power. If you think it important to do all the work yourself, you will waste energy and burn yourself out. Find people with the skills and creativity you lack. Either hire them, while putting your own name on top of theirs, or find a way to take their work and make it your own. Their creativity thus becomes yours, and you seem a genius to the world.

There is another application of this law that does not require the parasitic use of your contemporaries' labor: Use the past, a vast storehouse of knowledge and wisdom. Isaac Newton called this "standing on the shoulders of giants." He meant that in making his discoveries he had built on the achievements of others. A great part of his aura of genius, he knew, was attributable to his shrewd ability to make the most of the insights of ancient, medieval, and Renaissance scientists. Shakespeare borrowed plots, characterizations, and even dialogue from Plutarch, among other writers, for he knew that nobody surpassed Plutarch in the writing of subtle psychology and witty quotes. How many later writers have in their turn borrowed from – *plagiarized* – Shakespeare?

Writers who have delved into human nature, ancient masters of strategy, historians of human stupidity and folly – their knowledge is gathering dust, waiting for you to come and stand on their shoulders. Their wit can be your wit, their skill can be your skill, and they will never come around to tell people how unoriginal you really are. You can

To be sure, if the hunter relies on the security of the carriage, utilizes the legs of the six horses, and makes Wang Liang hold their reins, then he will not tire himself and will find it easy to overtake swift animals. Now supposing he discarded the advantage of the carriage, gave up the useful legs of the horses and the skill of Wang Liang, and alighted to run after the animals, then even though his legs were as quick as Liu Chi's, he would not be in time to overtake the animals. In fact, if good horses and strong carriages are taken into use, then mere bondmen and bondwomen will be good enough to catch the animals.

HAN FEI TZU,
CHINESE
PHILOSOPHER,
3RD CENTURY B.C.

slog through life, making endless mistakes, wasting time and energy trying to do things from your own experience. Or you can use the armies of the past. As Bismarck once said, "Fools say that they learn by experience. I prefer to profit by others' experience."

Image: The Vulture. Of all the creatures in the jungle, he has it the easiest. The hard work of others becomes his work; their failure to survive becomes his nourishment. Keep an eye on the Vulture – while you are hard at work, he is circling above. Do not fight him, join him.

Authority: There is much to be known, life is short, and life is not life without knowledge. It is therefore an excellent device to acquire knowledge from everybody. Thus, by the sweat of another's brow, you win the reputation of being an oracle. (Baltasar Gracian, 1601–1658)

MAKE OTHER PEOPLE
COME TO YOU –
USE BAIT IF NECESSARY

JUDGMENT

When you force the other person to act, you are the one in control. It is always better to make your opponent come to you, abandoning his own plans in the process. Lure him with fabulous gains – then attack. You hold the cards.

When I have laid
bait for deer, I
don't shoot at
the first doe that
comes to sniff,
but wait until the
whole herd has
gathered round.

OTTO VON
BISMARCK,
1815–1898

KEYS TO POWER

How many times has this scenario played itself out in history: An aggressive leader initiates a series of bold moves that begin by bringing him much power. Slowly, however, his power reaches a peak, and soon everything turns against him. His numerous enemies band together; trying to maintain his power, he exhausts himself going in this direction and that, and inevitably he collapses. The reason for this pattern is that the aggressive person is rarely in full control. He cannot see more than a couple of moves ahead, cannot see the consequences of this bold move or that one. Because he is constantly being forced to react to the moves of his ever growing host of enemies, and to the unforeseen consequences of his own rash actions, his aggressive energy is turned against him.

In the realm of power, you must ask yourself, What is the point of chasing here and there, trying to solve problems and defeat my enemies, if I never feel in control? Why am I always having to react to events instead of directing them? The answer is simple: Your idea of power is wrong. You have mistaken aggressive action for effective action. And most often the most effective action is to stay back, keep calm, and let others be frustrated by the traps you lay for them, playing for longterm power rather than quick victory.

Remember: The essence of power is the ability to keep the initiative, to get others to react to *your* moves, to keep your opponent and those around you on the defensive. When you make other people come to you,

you suddenly become the one controlling the situation. And the one who has control has power. Two things must happen to place you in this position: You yourself must learn to master your emotions, and never to be influenced by anger; meanwhile, however, you must play on people's natural tendency to react angrily when pushed and baited. In the long run, the ability to make others come to you is a weapon far more powerful than any tool of aggression.

One added benefit of making the opponent come to you is that it forces him to operate in your territory. Being on hostile ground will make him nervous and often he will rush his actions and make mistakes. For negotiations or meetings, it is always wise to lure others into your territory, or the territory of your choice. You have your bearings, while they see nothing familiar and are subtly placed on the defensive.

Manipulation is a dangerous game. Once someone suspects he is being manipulated, it becomes harder and harder to control him. But when you make your opponent come to you, you create the illusion that he is controlling the situation.

The great nineteenth-century robber baron Daniel Drew was a master at playing the stock market. When he wanted a particular stock to be bought or sold, driving prices up or down, he rarely resorted to the direct approach. One of his tricks was to hurry through an exclusive club near Wall Street, obviously on his way to the stock exchange, and to pull out his customary red bandanna to wipe his perspiring brow. A slip of paper would fall from this bandanna that he would pretend not to notice. The club's members were always trying to foresee Drew's moves, and they would pounce on the paper, which invariably seemed to contain an inside tip on a stock. Word would spread, and members would buy or sell the stock in droves, playing perfectly into Drew's hands.

Everything depends on the sweetness of your bait. If your trap is attractive enough, the turbulence of your enemies' emotions and desires will blind them to reality. The greedier they become, the more they can be led around.

Image: The Honeyed Bear Trap. The bear hunter does not chase his prey; a bear that knows it is hunted is nearly impossible to catch, and is ferocious if cornered. Instead, the hunter lays traps baited with honey. He does not exhaust himself and risk his life in pursuit. He baits, then waits.

Authority: Good warriors make others come to them, and do not go to others. This is the principle of emptiness and fullness of others and self. When you induce opponents to come to you, then their force is always empty; as long as you do not go to them, your force is always full. Attacking emptiness with fullness is like throwing stones on eggs. (Zhang Yu, 11th century commentator on *The Art of War*)

WIN THROUGH YOUR ACTIONS, NEVER THROUGH ARGUMENT

JUDGMENT

Any momentary triumph you think you have gained through argument is really a Pyrrhic victory: The resentment and ill will you stir up are stronger and last longer than any momentary change of opinion. It is much more powerful to get others to agree with you through your actions, without saying a word. Demonstrate, do not explicate.

KEYS TO POWER

In the realm of power you must learn to judge your moves by their long-term effects on other people. The problem in trying to prove a point or gain a victory through argument is that in the end you can never be certain how it affects the people you're arguing with: They may appear to agree with you politely, but inside they may resent you. Or perhaps something you said inadvertently even offended them – words have that insidious ability to be interpreted according to the other person's mood and insecurities. Even the best argument has no solid foundation, for we have all come to distrust the slippery nature of words. And days after agreeing with someone, we often revert to our old opinion out of sheer habit.

Understand this: Words are a dime a dozen. Everyone knows that in the heat of an argument we will all say anything to support our cause. We will quote the Bible, refer to unverifiable statistics. Who can be persuaded by bags of air like that? Action and demonstration are much more powerful and meaningful. They are there, before our eyes, for us to see. There are no offensive words, no possibility of misinterpretation. No one can argue with a demonstrated proof. As Baltasar Gracian remarks, "The truth is generally seen, rarely heard."

Sir Christopher Wren was England's version of the Renaissance man. He had mastered the sciences of mathematics, astronomy, physics, and physiology. Yet during his extremely long career as England's most celebrated architect he was often told by his patrons to make impractical changes in his designs. Never once did he argue or offend. He had other ways of proving his point.

In 1688, Wren designed a magnificent town hall for the city of Westminster. The mayor, however, was not satisfied; in fact he was nervous. He told Wren he was afraid the second floor was not secure, and that it could all come crashing down on his office on the first floor. He demanded that Wren add two stone columns for extra support. Wren, the consummate engineer, knew that these columns would serve no purpose, and that the mayor's fears were baseless. But build them he did, and the mayor was grateful. It was only years later that workmen on a high scaffold saw that the columns stopped just short of the ceiling.

They were dummies. But both men got what they wanted: The mayor could relax, and Wren knew posterity would understand that his original design worked and the columns were unnecessary.

The power of demonstrating your idea is that your opponents do not get defensive, and are therefore more open to persuasion. Making them literally and physically feel your meaning is infinitely more powerful than argument.

When aiming for power, or trying to conserve it, always look for the indirect route. And also choose your battles carefully. If it does not matter in the long run whether the other person agrees with you – or if time and their own experience will make them understand what you mean – then it is best not even to bother with a demonstration. Save your energy and walk away.

he then set up in what he thought the most suitable spot in the city. The Egyptians, constantly coming upon the statue, treated it with profound reverence, and as soon as Amasis heard of the effect it had upon them, he called a meeting and revealed the fact that the deeply revered statue was once a foot-bath, which they washed their feet and pissed and vomited in. He went on to say that his own case was much the same, in that once he had been only an ordinary person and was now their king; so that just as they had come to revere the transformed foot-bath, so they had better pay honor and respect to him too. In this way the Egyptians

Image: The Seesaw. Up and down and up and down go the arguers, getting nowhere fast. Get off the seesaw and show them your meaning without kicking or pushing. Leave them at the top and let gravity bring them gently to the ground.

Authority: Never argue. In society nothing must be discussed; give only results. (Benjamin Disraeli, 1804–1881)

INFECTION: AVOID THE

UNHAPPY AND UNLUCKY

JUDGMENT

You can die from someone else's misery – emotional states are as infectious as diseases. You may feel you are helping the drowning man but you are only precipitating your own disaster. The unfortunate sometimes draw misfortune on themselves; they will also draw it on you. Associate with the happy and fortunate instead.

*A nut found
itself carried by a
crow to the top
of a tall
campanile, and
by falling into a
crevice
succeeded in
escaping its
dread fate. It
then besought
the wall to
shelter it, by
appealing to it
by the grace of
God, and
praising its
height, and the
beauty and
noble tone of its
bells. "Alas," it
went on, "as I
have not been
able to drop
beneath the
green branches
of my old Father
and to lie in the
fallow earth
covered by his
fallen leaves, do
you, at least, not
abandon me.
When I found
myself in the
beak of the cruel
crow I made a
vow, that if I
escaped I would
end my life in a
little hole."*

KEYS TO POWER

Those misfortunates among us who have been brought down by circumstances beyond their control deserve all the help and sympathy we can give them. But there are others who are not born to misfortune or unhappiness, but who draw it upon themselves by their destructive actions and unsettling effect on others. It would be a great thing if we could raise them up, change their patterns, but more often than not it is their patterns that end up getting inside and changing us. The reason is simple – humans are extremely susceptible to the moods, emotions, and even the ways of thinking of those with whom they spend their time.

Understand this: In the game of power, the people you associate with are critical. The risk of associating with infectors is that you will waste valuable time and energy trying to free yourself. Through a kind of guilt by association, you will also suffer in the eyes of others. Never underestimate the dangers of infection.

There is only one solution to infection: quarantine. The danger is that these infecting types often present themselves as victims, making it difficult, at first, to see their miseries as self-inflicted. By the time you recognize the problem it is often too late. How you protect yourself against such insidious viruses? The answer lies in judging people on the effects they have on the world and not on the reasons they give for their problems. Infectors can be recognized by the misfortune they draw on themselves, their turbulent past, their long line of broken relationships, their unstable careers, and the very force of their character, which sweeps you up and makes you lose your reason. Be forewarned by these signs of an infector; learn to see the discontent in their eye. Most important of all, do not take pity. Do not enmesh yourself in trying to help. Flee the infector's presence or suffer the consequences.

The other side of infection is equally valid, and perhaps more readily understood: There are people who attract happiness to themselves by their good cheer, natural buoyancy, and intelligence. They are a source of pleasure, and you must associate with them to share in the prosperity they draw upon themselves.

This applies to more than good cheer and success: All positive qualities can infect us. Talleyrand had many strange and intimidating traits, but most agreed that he surpassed all Frenchmen in graciousness, aristocratic charm, and wit. Indeed he came from one of the oldest noble families in the country, and despite his belief in democracy and the French Republic, he retained his courtly manners. His contemporary Napoleon was in many ways the opposite – a peasant from Corsica, taciturn and ungracious, even violent.

There was no one Napoleon admired more than Talleyrand, and as best he could, he kept Talleyrand around him, hoping to

Image: A Virus. Unseen, it enters your pores without warning, spreading silently and slowly. Before you are aware of the infection, it is deep inside you.

At these words, the wall, moved with compassion, was content to shelter the nut in the spot where it had fallen. Within a short time, the nut burst open: its roots reached in between the crevices of the stones and began to push them apart; its shoots pressed up toward the sky. They soon rose above the building, and as the twisted roots grew thicker they began to thrust the walls apart and force the ancient stones from their old places. Then the wall, too late and in vain, bewailed the cause of its destruction, and in short time it fell in ruin.

LEONARDO DA VINCI, 1452–1519

soak up the culture he lacked. There is no doubt that Napoleon changed as his rule continued. Many of the rough edges were smoothed by his constant association with Talleyrand.

Use the positive side of this emotional osmosis to advantage. If, for example, you are miserly by nature, associate with the generous and they will infect you, opening up everything that is tight and restricted in you. If you are gloomy, gravitate to the cheerful. If you are prone to isolation, force yourself to befriend the gregarious. Never associate with those who share your defects – they will reinforce everything that holds you back. Only create associations with positive affinities. Make this a rule of life and you will benefit more than from all the therapy in the world.

Authority: Recognize the fortunate so that you may choose their company, and the unfortunate so that you may avoid them. Misfortune is usually the crime of folly, and among those who suffer from it there is no malady more contagious: never open your door to the least of misfortunes, for, if you do, many others will follow in its train ... Do not die of another's misery. (Baltasar Gracian, 1601–1658)

LEARN TO KEEP PEOPLE
DEPENDENT ON YOU

JUDGMENT

To maintain your independence you must always be needed and wanted. The more you are relied on, the more freedom you have. Make people depend on you for their happiness and prosperity and you have nothing to fear. Never teach them enough so that they can do without you.

KEYS TO POWER

The ultimate power is the power to get people to do as you wish. When you can do this
without having to force people or hurt them,
when they willingly grant you what you
desire, then your power is untouchable. The
best way to achieve this position is to create
a relationship of dependence. The master
requires your services; he is weak, or unable
to function without you; you have enmeshed
yourself in his work so deeply that doing
away with you would bring him great difficulty, or at least would mean valuable time
lost in training another to replace you. Once
such a relationship is established you have
the upper hand, the leverage to make the
master do as you wish. It is the classic case of
the man behind the throne, the servant of the
king who actually controls the king.

Do not be one of the many who mistakenly believe that the ultimate form of power
is independence. Power involves a relationship between people; you will always need
others as allies, pawns, or even as weak masters who serve as your front.

If you create no need for yourself, then
you will be done away with at the first opportunity. Someone younger, fresher, less
expensive, less threatening will replace you.
Do not take such a chance; make others
dependent on you. To get rid of you might
spell disaster, and your master dares not
tempt fate by finding out. There are many
ways to obtain such a position. Foremost
among them is to possess a talent and creative skill that simply cannot be replaced.

You do not have to be a genius; you do
have to have a skill that sets you apart from

the crowd. You should create a situation in which you can always latch on to another master or patron but your master cannot easily find another servant with your particular talent. And if, in reality, you are not actually indispensable, you must find a way to make it look as if you are. Having the appearance of specialized knowledge and skill gives you leeway in your ability to deceive those above you into thinking they cannot do without you.

Henry Kissinger managed to survive the many bloodlettings that went on in the Nixon White House not because he was the best diplomat Nixon could find – there were other fine negotiators – and not because the two men got along so well: they did not. Nor did they share their beliefs and politics. Kissinger survived because he entrenched himself in so many areas of the political structure that to do away with him would lead to chaos. He got himself involved in so many aspects and departments of the administration that his involvement became a card in his hand. It also made him many allies. If you can arrange such a position for yourself, getting rid of you becomes dangerous – all sorts of interdependencies will unravel.

One last warning: Do not imagine that your master's dependence on you will make him love you. In fact he may resent and fear you – but, as Machiavelli said, it is better to be feared than loved. Fear you can control; love, never. Depending on an emotion as subtle and changeable as love or friendship will only make you insecure. Better to have others depend on you out of fear of the consequences of losing you than out of love of your company.

Thus a wise prince will think of ways to keep his citizens of every sort and under every circumstance dependent on the state and on him; and then they will always be trustworthy.

NICCOLÒ
MACHIAVELLI,
1469–1527

Image: Vines with Many Thorns.
Below, the roots grow deep and wide. Above, the vines push through bushes, entwine themselves around trees and poles and window ledges. To get rid of them would cost such toil and blood, it is easier to let them climb.

Authority: Make people depend on you. More is to be gained from such dependence than courtesy. He who has slaked his thirst immediately turns his back on the well, no longer needing it. When dependence disappears, so does civility and decency, and then respect. The first lesson which experience should teach you is to keep hope alive but never satisfied, keeping even a royal patron ever in need of you. (Baltasar Gracian, 1601–1658)

USE SELECTIVE HONESTY
AND GENEROSITY TO
DISARM YOUR VICTIM

JUDGMENT

One sincere and honest move will cover over dozens of dishonest ones. Open-hearted gestures of honesty and generosity bring down the guard of even the most suspicious people. Once your selective honesty opens a hole in their armor, you can deceive and manipulate them at will. A timely gift – a Trojan horse – will serve the same purpose.

*Francesco
Giuseppe Borri
of Milan, whose
death in 1695 fell
just within the
seventeenth
century ... was a
forerunner of
that special type
of charlatanical
adventurer, the
courtier or
"cavalier"
impostor ... His
real period of
glory began after
he moved to
Amsterdam.
There he
assumed the title
of* Medico
Universale, *maintained a
great retinue,
and drove about
in a coach with
six horses ...
Patients
streamed to him,
and some
invalids had
themselves
carried in sedan
chairs all the
way from Paris
to his place in
Amsterdam.
Borri took no
payment for his
consultations; he*

KEYS TO POWER

The essence of deception is distraction. Distracting the people you want to deceive gives you the time and space to do something they won't notice. An act of kindness, generosity or honesty is the most powerful form of distraction because it disarms other people's suspicions. It turns them into children, eagerly lapping up any kind of affectionate gesture.

In ancient China this was called "giving before you take" – the giving makes it hard for the other person to notice the taking. It is a device with infinite practical uses. Brazenly taking something from someone is dangerous, even for the powerful. The victim will plot revenge. It is also dangerous simply to ask for what you need, no matter how politely: Unless the other person sees some gain for themselves, they may come to resent your neediness. Learn to give before you take. It softens the ground, takes the bite out of a future request, or simply creates a distraction. And the giving can take many forms: an actual gift, a generous act, a kind favor, an "honest" admission – whatever it takes.

Selective honesty is best employed on your first encounter with someone. We are all creatures of habit, and our first impressions last a long time. If someone believes you are honest at the start of your relationship it takes a lot to convince them otherwise. This gives you room to maneuver.

A single act of honesty is often not enough. What is required is a reputation for honesty, built on a series of acts – but these can be quite inconsequential. Once this reputation is established, as with first impressions, it is hard to shake.

In ancient China, Duke Wu of Chêng decided it was time to take over the increasingly powerful kingdom of Hu. Telling no one of his plan, he married his daughter to Hu's ruler. He then called a council and asked his ministers, "I am considering a military campaign. Which country should we invade?" As he had expected, one of his ministers replied, "Hu should be invaded." The duke seemed angry, and said, "Hu is a sister state now. Why do you suggest invading her?" He had the minister executed for his impolitic remark. The ruler of Hu heard about this, and considering other tokens of Wu's honesty and the marriage with his daughter, he took no precautions to defend himself from Chêng. A few weeks later, Chêng forces swept through Hu and took the country, never to relinquish it.

Honesty is one of the best ways to disarm the wary, but it is not the only one. Any kind of noble, apparently selfless act will serve. Perhaps the best such act, though, is one of generosity. Few people can resist a gift, even from the most hardened enemy, which is why it is often the perfect way to disarm people. A gift brings out the child in us, instantly lowering our defenses. Although we often view other people's actions in the most cynical light, we rarely see the Machiavellian element of a gift, which quite often hides ulterior motives. A gift is the perfect object in which to hide a deceptive move.

This tactic must be practiced with caution: If people see through it, their disappointed feelings of gratitude and warmth will

distributed great sums among the poor and was never known to receive any money through the post or bills of exchange. As he continued to live with such splendor, nevertheless, it was presumed that he possessed the philosophers' stone. Suddenly this benefactor disappeared from Amsterdam. Then it was discovered that he had taken with him money and diamonds that had been placed in his charge.

GRETE DE FRANCESCO, THE POWER OF THE CHARLATAN, 1939

become the most violent hatred and distrust. Unless you can make the gesture seem sincere and heartfelt, do not play with fire.

Image: The Trojan Horse. Your guile is hidden inside a magnificent gift that proves irresistible to your opponent. The walls open. Once inside, wreak havoc.

Authority: When Duke Hsien of Chin was about to raid Yü, he presented to them a jade and a team of horses. When Earl Chih was about to raid Ch'ou-yu, he presented to them grand chariots. Hence the saying: "When you are about to take, you should give." (Han Fei Tzu, Chinese philosopher, third century B.C.)

WHEN ASKING FOR HELP, APPEAL TO PEOPLE'S SELF-INTEREST, NEVER TO THEIR MERCY OR GRATITUDE

JUDGMENT

If you need to turn to an ally for help, do not bother to remind him of your past assistance and good deeds. He will find a way to ignore you. Instead, uncover something in your request, or in your alliance with him, that will benefit him, and emphasize it out of all proportion. He will respond enthusiastically when he sees something to be gained for himself.

*A peasant had in
his garden an
apple-tree, which
bore no fruit, but
only served as a
perch for the
sparrows and
grasshoppers. He
resolved to cut it
down, and,
taking his ax in
hand, made a
bold stroke at its
roots. The
grasshoppers
and sparrows
entreated him
not to cut down
the tree that
sheltered them,
but to spare it,
and they would
sing to him and
lighten his
labors. He paid
no attention to
their request, but
gave the tree a
second and a
third blow with
his axe. When he
reached the
hollow of the
tree, he found a
hive full of
honey. Having
tasted the
honeycomb, he
threw down his
ax, and, looking*

KEYS TO POWER

In your quest for power, you will constantly find yourself in the position of asking for help from those more powerful than you. There is an art to asking for help, an art that depends on your ability to understand the person you are dealing with, and to not confuse your needs with theirs.

Most people never succeed at this, because they are completely trapped in their own wants and desires. They start from the assumption that the people they are appealing to have a selfless interest in helping them. They talk as if their needs mattered to these people – who probably couldn't care less. Sometimes they refer to larger issues: a great cause, or grand emotions such as love and gratitude. They go for the big picture when simple, everyday realities would have much more appeal. What they do not realize is that even the most powerful person is locked inside needs of his own, and that if you make no appeal to his self-interest, he merely sees you as desperate or, at best, a waste of time.

A key step in the process is to understand the other person's psychology. Is he vain? Is he concerned about his reputation or his social standing? Does he have enemies you could help him vanquish? Is he simply motivated by money and power?

When the Mongols invaded China in the twelfth century, they threatened to obliterate a culture that had thrived for over two thousand years. Their leader, Genghis Khan, saw nothing in China but a country that lacked pasturing for his horses, and he decided to destroy the place, leveling all its cities, for "it would be better to exterminate the Chinese and let the grass grow." It was not a soldier, a general, or a king who saved the Chinese from devastation, but a man named Yelu Ch'u-Ts'ai. A foreigner himself, Ch'u-Ts'ai had come to appreciate the superiority of Chinese culture. He managed to make himself a trusted adviser to Genghis Khan, and persuaded him that he would reap riches out of the place if, instead of destroying it, he simply taxed everyone who lived there. Khan saw the wisdom in this and did as Ch'u-Ts'ai advised.

When Khan took the city of Kaifeng, after a long siege, and decided to massacre its inhabitants (as he had in other cities that had resisted him), Ch'u-Ts'ai told him that the finest craftsmen and engineers in China had fled to Kaifeng, and it would be better to put them to use. Kaifeng was spared. Never before had Genghis Khan shown such mercy, but then it really wasn't mercy that saved Kaifeng. Ch'u-Ts'ai knew Khan well. He was a barbaric peasant who cared nothing for culture, or indeed for anything other than warfare and practical results. Ch'u-Ts'ai chose to appeal to the only emotion that would work on such a man: greed.

Self-interest is the lever that will move people. Once you make them see how you can in some way meet their needs or advance their cause, their resistance to your requests for help will magically fall away. At each step on the way to acquiring power, you must train yourself to think your way inside the other person's mind, to see their needs and interests, to get rid of the screen of your own feelings that obscure the truth. Master this art and there will be no limits to what you can accomplish.

on the tree as sacred, took great care of it. Self-interest alone moves some men.

FABLES, AESOP,
LATE SIXTH
CENTURY B.C.

Image: A Cord that Binds. The cord of mercy and gratitude is threadbare, and will break at the first shock. Do not throw such a lifeline. The cord of mutual self-interest is woven of many fibers and cannot easily be severed. It will serve you well for years.

Authority: The shortest and best way to make your fortune is to let people see clearly that it is in their interests to promote yours. (Jean de La Bruyère, 1645–1696)

POSE AS A FRIEND,

WORK AS A SPY

JUDGMENT

Knowing about your rival is critical. Use spies to gather valuable information that will keep you a step ahead. Better still: Play the spy yourself. In polite social encounters, learn to probe. Ask indirect questions to get people to reveal their weaknesses and intentions. There is no occasion that is not an opportunity for artful spying.

In the realm of power, your goal is a degree of control over future events. Part of the problem you face, then, is that people won't tell you all their thoughts, emotions, and plans. Carefully controlling what they say, they often keep the most critical parts of their character hidden – their weaknesses, ulterior motives, obsessions. The result is that you cannot predict their moves, and are constantly in the dark. The trick is to find a way to probe them, to find out their secrets and hidden intentions, without letting them know what you are up to.

This is not as difficult as you might think. A friendly front will let you secretly gather information on friends and enemies alike. Let others consult the horoscope or read tarot cards: You have more concrete means of seeing into the future.

The most common way of spying is to use other people. The method is simple, powerful, but risky: You will certainly gather information, but you have little control over the people who are doing the work. Perhaps they will ineptly reveal your spying, or even secretly turn against you. It is far better to be the spy yourself, to pose as a friend while secretly gathering information.

The French politician Talleyrand was one of the greatest practitioners of this art. He had an uncanny ability to worm secrets out of people in polite conversation. Throughout Talleyrand's life, people said he was a superb conversationalist – yet he actually said very little. He never talked about his own ideas; he got others to reveal theirs. He would blurt out what seemed to be a secret

If you have reason to suspect that a person is telling you a lie, look as though you believed every word he said. This will give him courage to go on; he will become more vehement in his assertions and in the end betray himself. Again, if you perceive that a person is trying to conceal something from you, but with only partial success, look as though you did not believe him. The opposition on your part will provoke him into leading out his reserve of truth and bringing the whole force of it to bear upon your incredulity.

ARTHUR SCHOPENHAUER, 1788–1860

(actually something he had made up), then watch his listeners' reactions.

During social gatherings and innocuous encounters, pay attention. This is when people's guards are down. By getting people to talk, you can make them reveal things. The brilliance of the maneuver is that they will mistake your interest in them for friendship, so that you not only learn, but you also make allies.

Nevertheless, you should practice this tactic with caution and care. If people begin to suspect you are worming secrets out of them under the cover of conversation, they will strictly avoid you. Emphasize friendly chatter, not valuable information. Your search for gems of information cannot be too obvious or your probing questions will reveal more about yourself and your intentions than about the information you hope to find.

A trick to try in spying comes from La Rochefoucauld, who wrote, "Sincerity is found in very few men, and is often the cleverest of ruses – one is sincere in order to draw out the confidence and secrets of the other." By pretending to bare your heart to another person, in other words, you make them more likely to reveal their own secrets. Give them a false confession and they will give you a real one. Another trick was identified by the philosopher Arthur Schopenhauer, who suggested vehemently contradicting people you're in conversation with as a way of irritating them, stirring them up so that they lose some of the control over their words. In their emotional reaction they will reveal all kinds of truths about themselves, truths you can later use against them.

Rulers see through spies, as cows through smell, Brahmins through scriptures and the rest of the people through their normal eyes.

KAUTILYA,
INDIAN
PHILOSOPHER,
THIRD CENTURY
B.C.

Image: The Third Eye of the Spy. In the land of the two-eyed, the third eye gives you the omniscience of a god. You see farther than others, and you see deeper into them. Nobody is safe from the eye but you.

Authority: Now the reason a brilliant sovereign and a wise general conquer the enemy whenever they move, and their achievements surpass those of ordinary men, is their foreknowledge of the enemy situation. This "foreknowledge" cannot be elicited from spirits, nor from gods, nor by analogy with past events, nor by astrologic calculations. It must be obtained from men who know the enemy situation – from spies. (Sun-tzu, *The Art of War*, fourth century B.C.)

LAW
15

CRUSH YOUR
ENEMY TOTALLY

JUDGMENT

*All great leaders since Moses have known that a feared
enemy must be crushed completely. (Sometimes they have
learned this the hard way.) If one ember is left alight, no
matter how dimly it smolders, a fire will eventually break
out. More is lost through stopping halfway than through
total annihilation: The enemy will recover, and will seek
revenge. Crush him, not only in body but in spirit.*

In your struggle for power you will stir up
rivalries and create enemies. There will be
people you cannot win over, who will
remain your enemies no matter what. Such
enemies wish you ill. There is nothing they
want more than to eliminate you. If, in your
struggles with them, you stop half- or even
three-quarters of the way, out of mercy or
hope of reconciliation, you only make them
more determined, more embittered, and
they will someday take revenge. They may
act friendly for the time being, but this is only
because you have defeated them. They have
no choice but to bide their time.

The solution: Have no mercy. Do not
take their hatred personally. Crush your enemies as totally as they would crush you. Ultimately the only peace and security you can
hope for from your enemies is their disap-
pearance.

Mao Tse-tung knew the importance of
this law. In 1934, the communist leader and
some 75,000 poorly equipped soldiers fled
into the desolate mountains of western
China to escape Chiang Kai-shek's much
larger army, in what has since been called
the Long March.

Chiang was determined to eliminate
every last communist, and by a few years
later Mao had less than 10,000 soldiers left.
By 1937, in fact, when China was invaded by
Japan, Chiang calculated that the communists were no longer a threat. He chose to
give up the chase and concentrate on the
Japanese. Ten years later the communists
had recovered enough to rout Chiang's
army. Chiang had forgotten the wisdom of

crushing the enemy; Mao had not. Chiang was pursued until he and his entire army fled to the island of Taiwan. Nothing remains of his regime in mainland China to this day.

The goal of total victory is an axiom of modern warfare, and was codified as such by Carl von Clausewitz, the premier philosopher of war. Analyzing the campaigns of Napoleon, von Clausewitz wrote, "We do claim that direct annihilation of the enemy's forces must always be the *dominant consideration* ... Once a major victory is achieved there must be no talk of rest, of breathing space ... but only of the pursuit, going for the enemy again, seizing his capital, attacking his reserves and anything else that might give his country aid and comfort." The reason for this is that after war come negotiation and the division of territory. If you have only won a partial victory, you will inevitably lose in negotiation what you have gained by war.

The solution is simple: Allow your enemies no options. Annihilate them and their territory is yours to carve. The goal of power is to control your enemies completely, to make them obey your will. You cannot afford to go halfway. If they have no options, they will be forced to do your bidding. This law has applications far beyond the battlefield. Negotiation is the insidious viper that will eat away at your victory, so give your enemies nothing to negotiate, no hope, no room to maneuver. They are crushed and that is that.

Be realistic: if you are not ruthless with your enemies, you will never be secure. And if you are not in a position to do away with them or banish them from your presence, at

To have ultimate victory, you must be ruthless.

NAPOLEON
BONAPARTE,
1769–1821

least understand that they are plotting against you, and pay no heed to whatever friendliness they feign. Your only weapon in such a situation is your own wariness.

Image: A Viper crushed beneath your foot, but left alive, will rear up and bite you with a double dose of venom. An enemy that is left around is like a half-dead viper that you nurse back to health. Time makes the venom grow stronger.

Authority: For it must be noted, that men must either be caressed or else annihilated; they will revenge themselves for small injuries, but cannot do so for great ones; the injury therefore that we do to a man must be such that we need not fear his vengeance. (Niccolò Machiavelli, 1469–1527)

USE ABSENCE TO INCREASE RESPECT AND HONOR

JUDGMENT

Too much circulation makes the price go down: The more you are seen and heard from, the more common you appear. If you are already established in a group, temporary withdrawal from it will make you more talked about, even more admired. You must learn when to leave. Create value through scarcity.

The first man
who saw a camel
fled;
The second
ventured within
distance;
The third dared
slip a halter
round its head.
Familiarity in
this existence
Makes all things
tame, for what
may seem
Terrible or
bizarre, when
once our eyes
Have had time to
acclimatize,
Becomes quite
commonplace.
Since I'm on this
theme,
I've heard of
sentinels posted
by the shore
Who, spotting
something far-
away afloat,
Couldn't resist
the shout:
"A sail! A sail!
A mighty man-
of-war!"
Five minutes
later it's a packet
boat,
And then a skiff,
and then a bale,
And finally some

KEYS TO POWER

Everything in the world depends on absence and presence. A strong presence will draw power and attention to you – you shine more brightly than those around you. But a point is inevitably reached where too much presence creates the opposite effect: The more you are seen and heard from, the more your value degrades. You become a habit. No matter how hard you try to be different, subtly, without your knowing why, people respect you less and less. At the right moment you must learn to withdraw yourself before they unconsciously push you away. It is a game of hide-and-seek.

The truth of this law can most easily be appreciated in matters of love and seduction. In the beginning stages of an affair, the lover's absence stimulates your imagination, forming a sort of aura around him or her. But this aura fades when you know too much – when your imagination no longer has room to roam. The loved one becomes a person like anyone else, a person whose presence is taken for granted.

To prevent this you need to starve the other person of your presence. Force their respect by threatening them with the possibility that they will lose you for good.

Napoleon was recognizing the law of absence and presence when he said, "If I am often seen at the theater, people will cease to notice me." Today, in a world inundated with presence through the flood of images, the game of withdrawal is all the more powerful. We rarely know when to withdraw any more, and nothing seems private, so we are awed by anyone who is able to disappear by choice. Novelists J. D. Salinger and Thomas Pynchon have created cultlike followings by knowing when to disappear.

Another, more everyday side of this law, but one that demonstrates its truth even further, is the law of scarcity in the science of economics. By withdrawing something from the market, you create instant value. In seventeenth-century Holland, the royal family wanted to make the tulip more than just a beautiful flower – they wanted it to be a kind of status symbol. Making the flower scarce, indeed almost impossible to obtain, they sparked what was later called tulipomania. A single flower was now worth more than its weight in gold.

Extend the law of scarcity to your own skills. Make what you are offering the world rare and hard to find, and you instantly increase its value.

There always comes a moment when those in power overstay their welcome. We have grown tired of them, lost respect for them; we see them as no different from the rest of mankind, which is to say that we see them as rather worse, since we inevitably compare their current status in our eyes to their former one. There is an art to knowing when to retire. If it is done right, you regain the respect you had lost, and retain a part of your power.

Make yourself too available and the aura of power you have created around yourself will wear away. Turn the game around: Make yourself less accessible and you increase the value of your presence.

sticks bobbing about.
I know of plenty such
To whom this story applies –
People whom distance magnifies,
Who, close to, don't amount to much.

LA FONTAINE, 1621–1695

Image: The Sun. It can only be appreciated by its absence. The longer the days of rain, the more the sun is craved. But too many hot days and the sun overwhelms. Learn to keep yourself obscure and make people demand your return.

Authority: Use absence to create respect and esteem. If presence diminishes fame, absence augments it. A man who when absent is regarded as a lion becomes when present something common and ridiculous. Talents lose their luster if we become too familiar with them, for the outer shell of the mind is more readily seen than its rich inner kernel. Even the outstanding genius makes use of retirement so that men may honor him and so that the yearning aroused by his absence may cause him to be esteemed. (Baltasar Gracian, 1601–1658)

KEEP OTHERS IN
SUSPENSE:
CULTIVATE AN AIR OF
UNPREDICTABILITY

JUDGMENT

Humans are creatures of habit with an insatiable need to see familiarity in other people's actions. Your predictability gives them a sense of control. Turn the tables: Be deliberately unpredictable. Behavior that seems to have no consistency or purpose will keep them off balance, and they will wear themselves out trying to explain your moves. Taken to an extreme, this strategy can intimidate and terrorize.

Nothing is more terrifying than the sudden and unpredictable. That is why we are so frightened by earthquakes and tornadoes: We do not know when they will strike. After one has occurred, we wait in terror for the next one. To a lesser degree, this is the effect that unpredictable human behavior has on us.

Animals behave in set patterns, which is why we are able to hunt and kill them. Only man has the capacity consciously to alter his behavior, to improvise and overcome the weight of routine and habit. Yet most men do not realize this power. They prefer the comforts of routine, of giving in to the animal nature that has them repeating the same compulsive actions time and time again. They do this because it requires no effort, and because they mistakenly believe that if they do not unsettle others, they will be left alone. Understand: A person of power instills a kind of fear by *deliberately* unsettling those around him to keep the initiative on his side. You sometimes need to strike without warning, to make others tremble when they least expect it. It is a device that the powerful have used for centuries.

Filippo Maria, the last of the Visconti dukes of Milan in fifteenth-century Italy, consciously did the opposite of what everyone expected of him. For instance, he might suddenly shower a courtier with attention, and then, once the man had come to expect a promotion to higher office, would suddenly start treating him with the utmost disdain. Confused, the man might leave the court, when the duke would suddenly recall

Life at court is a serious, melancholy game of chess, which requires us to draw up our pieces and batteries, form a plan, pursue it, parry that of our adversary. Sometimes, however, it is better to take risks and play the most capricious, unpredictable move.

JEAN DE LA
BRUYÈRE,
1645–1696

him and start treating him well again. Doubly confused, the courtier would wonder whether his assumption that he would be promoted had become obvious, and offensive, to the duke, and would start to behave as if he no longer expected such honor. The duke would rebuke him for his lack of ambition, and would send him away.

The secret of dealing with Filippo was simple: Do not presume to know what he wants. Do not try to guess what will please him. Never inject your will; just surrender to his will. Then wait to see what happens. Amidst the confusion and uncertainty he created, the duke ruled supreme, unchallenged and at peace.

People are always trying to read the motives behind your actions, and to use your predictability against you. Throw in a completely inexplicable move and you put them on the defensive.

For a while, Pablo Picasso worked with the art dealer Paul Rosenberg, then one day, for no apparent reason, he told the man he would no longer give him any work to sell. As Picasso explained, "Rosenberg would spend the next forty-eight hours trying to figure out why. Was I reserving things for some other dealer? I'd go on working and sleeping and Rosenberg would spend his time figuring. In two days he'd come back, nerves jangled, anxious, saying, 'After all, dear friend, you wouldn't turn me down if I offered you this much [naming a substantially higher figure] for those paintings rather than the price I've been accustomed to paying you, would you?'"

Unpredictability is not only a weapon of

Always mystify, mislead, and surprise the enemy, if possible ... such tactics will win every time and a small army may thus destroy a large one.

GENERAL STONEWALL JACKSON, 1824–1863

terror: Scrambling your patterns on a day-to-day basis will cause a stir around you and stimulate interest. People will talk about you, ascribe motives and explanations that have nothing to do with the truth, but that keep you constantly in their minds. In the end, the more capricious you appear, the more respect you will garner. Only the terminally subordinate act in a predictable manner.

Image: A Wind that cannot be foreseen. Sudden shifts in the barometer, inexplicable changes in direction and velocity. There is no defense: a cyclone sows terror and confusion.

Authority: The enlightened ruler is so mysterious that he seems to dwell nowhere, so inexplicable that no one can seek him. He reposes in nonaction above, and his ministers tremble below. (Han Fei Tzu, Chinese philosopher, third century B.C.)

LAW

18

DO NOT BUILD
FORTRESSES TO PROTECT
YOURSELF – ISOLATION
IS DANGEROUS

JUDGMENT

The world is dangerous and enemies are everywhere –
everyone has to protect themselves. A fortress seems the
safest. But isolation exposes you to more dangers than it
protects you from – it cuts you off from valuable infor-
mation, it makes you conspicuous and an easy target.
Better to circulate among people, find allies, mingle. You
are shielded from your enemies by the crowd.

Machiavelli makes the argument that in a strictly military sense a fortress is invariably a mistake. It becomes a symbol of power's isolation, and is an easy target for its builders' enemies. Designed to defend you, fortresses actually cut you off from help and cut into your flexibility. They may appear impregnable, but once you retire to one, everyone knows where you are; and a siege does not have to succeed to turn your fortress into a prison. With their small and confined spaces, fortresses are also extremely vulnerable to the plague and contagious diseases. In a strategic sense, the isolation of a fortress provides no protection, and actually creates more problems than it solves.

Because humans are social creatures by nature, power depends on social interaction and circulation. To make yourself powerful you must place yourself at the center of things. All activity should revolve around you, and you should be aware of everything happening on the street, and of anyone who might be hatching plots against you. The danger for most people comes when they feel threatened. In such times they tend to retreat and close ranks, to find security in a kind of fortress. In doing so, however, they come to rely for information on a smaller and smaller circle, and lose perspective on events around them. They lose maneuverability and become easy targets, and their isolation makes them paranoid. As in warfare and most games of strategy, isolation often precedes defeat and death.

In moments of uncertainty and danger, you need to fight this desire to turn inward.

Solitude is dangerous to reason, without being favorable to virtue ... Remember that the solitary mortal is certainly luxurious, probably superstitious, and possibly mad.

DR SAMUEL JOHNSON, 1709–1784

Instead, make yourself more accessible, seek out old allies and make new ones, force yourself into more and more different circles. This has been the trick of powerful people for centuries.

The Roman statesman Cicero was born into the lower nobility, and had little chance of power unless he managed to make a place for himself among the aristocrats who controlled the city. He succeeded brilliantly, identifying everyone with influence and figuring out how they were connected to one another. He mingled everywhere, knew everyone, and had such a vast network of connections that an enemy here could easily be counterbalanced by an ally there.

Since humans are such social creatures, it follows that the social arts that make us pleasant to be around can only be practiced by constant exposure and circulation. The more you are in contact with others, the more graceful and at ease you become. Isolation, on the other hand, engenders an awkwardness in your gestures, and leads to further isolation, as people start avoiding you.

Instead of falling into the fortress mentality, view the world in the following manner: It is like a vast palace, with every room communicating with another. You need to be permeable, able to float in and out of different circles and mix with different types. That kind of mobility and social contact will protect you from plotters, who will be unable to keep secrets from you, and from your enemies, who will be unable to isolate you from your allies. Always on the move, you mix and mingle in the rooms of the palace, never

The king [Louis XIV] not only saw to it that all the high nobility was present at his court, he demanded the same of minor nobility. At his lever and coucher, at his meals, in his gardens of Versailles, he always looked about him, noticing everything. He was offended if the most distinguished nobles did not live permanently at court, and those who showed themselves never or hardly ever incurred his full displeasure. If one of these desired something, the king would say proudly: "I do not know him," and the judgement was irrevocable.

DUC DE SAINT SIMON, 1675–1755

sitting or settling in one place. No hunter can fix his aim on such a swift-moving creature.

Image: The Fortress. High up on the hill, the citadel becomes a symbol of all that is hateful in power and authority. The citizens of the town betray you to the first enemy that comes. Cut off from communication and intelligence, the citadel falls with ease.

Authority: A good and wise prince, desirous of maintaining that character, and to avoid giving the opportunity to his sons to become oppressive, will never build fortresses, so that they may place their reliance upon the good will of their subjects, and not upon the strength of citadels. (Niccolò Machiavelli, 1469–1527)

KNOW WHO YOU'RE
DEALING WITH –
DO NOT OFFEND THE
WRONG PERSON

JUDGMENT

*There are many different kinds of people in the world,
and you can never assume that everyone will react to
your strategies in the same way. Deceive or outmaneuver
some people and they will spend the rest of their lives seek-
ing revenge. They are wolves in lambs' clothing. Choose
your victims and opponents carefully, then – never
offend or deceive the wrong person.*

OPPONENTS, SUCKERS, AND VICTIMS

In your rise to power you will come across many breeds of opponent, sucker, and victim. The highest form of the art of power is the ability to distinguish the wolves from the lambs, the foxes from the hares, the hawks from the vultures. If you make this distinction well, you will succeed without needing to coerce anyone too much. But if you deal blindly with whoever crosses your path, you will have a life of constant sorrow, if you even live that long. Being able to recognize types of people, and to act accordingly, is critical. The following are the five most dangerous and difficult types of mark in the jungle.

The Arrogant and Proud Man. Although he may initially disguise it, this man's touchy pride makes him very dangerous. Any perceived slight will lead to a vengeance of overwhelming violence. You may say to yourself, "But I only said such-and-such at a party, where everyone was drunk ..." It does not matter. There is no sanity behind his overreaction, so do not waste time trying to figure him out. If at any point in your dealings with a person you sense an oversensitive and overactive pride, flee. Whatever you are hoping for from him isn't worth it.

The Hopelessly Insecure Man. This man is related to the proud and arrogant type, but is less violent and harder to spot. His ego is fragile, his sense of self insecure, and if he feels himself deceived or attacked, the hurt will simmer. He will attack you in bites that will take forever to get big enough for you to notice. If you find you have deceived or harmed such a man, disappear for a long time. Do not stay around him or he will nibble you to death.

Mr Suspicion. Another variant on the breeds above, this is a future Joe Stalin. He sees what he wants to see – usually the worst – in other people, and imagines that everyone is after him. Mr Suspicion is in fact the least dangerous of the three: Genuinely unbalanced, he is easy to deceive, just as Stalin himself was constantly deceived. Play on his suspicious nature to get him to turn against other people. But if you do become the target of his suspicions, watch out.

The Serpent with a Long Memory. If hurt or deceived, this man will show no anger on the surface; he will calculate and wait. Then, when he is in a position to turn the tables, he will exact a revenge marked by a cold-blooded shrewdness. Recognize this man by his calculation and cunning in the different areas of his life. He is usually cold and unaffectionate. Be doubly careful of this snake, and if you have somehow injured him, either crush him completely or get him out of your sight.

The Plain, Unassuming, and Often Unintelligent Man. Ah, your ears prick up when you find such a tempting victim. But this man is a lot harder to deceive than you imagine. Falling for a ruse often takes intelligence and imagination – a sense of the possible rewards. The blunt man will not take the bait

THE CROW AND THE SHEEP

A troublesome Crow seated herself on the back of a Sheep. The Sheep, much against his will, carried her backward and forward for a long time, and at last said, "If you had treated a dog in this way, you would have had your deserts from his sharp teeth." To this the Crow replied, "I despise the weak, and yield to the strong. I know whom I may bully, and whom I must flatter; and thus I hope to prolong my life to a good old age."

FABLES, AESOP, LATE SIXTH CENTURY B.C.

because he does not recognize it. He is that unaware. The danger with this man is not that he will harm you or seek revenge, but merely that he will waste your time, energy, resources, and even your sanity in trying to deceive him. Have a test ready for a mark – a joke, a story. If his reaction is utterly literal, this is the type you are dealing with. Continue at your own risk.

Image: The Hunter. He does not lay the same trap for a wolf as for a fox. He does not set bait where no one will take it. He knows his prey thoroughly, its habits and hideaways, and hunts accordingly.

Authority: Be convinced, that there are no persons so insignificant and inconsiderable, but may, some time or other, have it in their power to be of use to you; which they certainly will not, if you have once shown them contempt. Wrongs are often forgiven, but contempt never is. Our pride remembers it for ever. (Lord Chesterfield, 1694–1773)

DO NOT COMMIT
TO ANYONE

JUDGMENT

It is the fool who always rushes to take sides. Do not commit to any side or cause but yourself. By maintaining your independence you become the master of others – playing people against one another, making them pursue you.

KEYS TO POWER

Since power depends greatly on appearances, you must learn the tricks that will enhance your image. Refusing to commit to a person or group is one of these. When you hold yourself back, you incur not anger but a kind of respect. You instantly seem powerful because you make yourself ungraspable, rather than succumbing to the group, or to the relationship, as most people do. This aura of power only grows with time: As your reputation for independence grows, more and more people will come to desire you, wanting to be the one who gets you to commit. Desire is like a virus: If we see that someone is desired by other people, we tend to find this person desirable too.

The moment you commit, the magic is gone. You become like everyone else. People will try all kinds of underhanded methods to get you to commit. They will give you gifts, shower you with favors, all to put you under obligation. Encourage the attention, stimulate their interest, but do not commit at any cost. Accept the gifts and favors if you so desire, but be careful to maintain your inner aloofness. You cannot inadvertently allow yourself to feel obligated to anyone.

Remember, though: The goal is not to put people off, or to make it seem that you are incapable of commitment. Like Queen Elizabeth I, the Virgin Queen, you need to stir the pot, excite interest, lure people with the possibility of having you. You have to bend to their attention occasionally, then – but never too far.

The Greek soldier and statesman Alcibiades played this game to perfection. It was

Alcibiades who inspired and led the massive Athenian armada that invaded Sicily in 414 B.C. When envious Athenians back home tried to bring him down by accusing him of trumped-up charges, he defected to the enemy, the Spartans, instead of facing a trial back home. Then, after the Athenians were defeated at Syracuse, he left Sparta for Persia, even though the power of Sparta was now on the rise. Now, however, both the Athenians and the Spartans courted Alcibiades because of his influence with the Persians; and the Persians showered him with honors because of his power over the Athenians and the Spartans. He made promises to every side but committed to none, and in the end he held all the cards.

If you aspire to power and influence, try the Alcibiades tactic: Put yourself in the middle between competing powers. Lure one side with the promise of your help; the other side, always wanting to outdo its enemy, will pursue you as well. As each side vies for your attention, you will immediately seem a person of great influence and desirability. More power will accrue to you than if you had rashly committed to one side.

In France's July Revolution of 1830, after three days of riots, the statesman Talleyrand, now elderly, sat by his Paris window, listening to the pealing bells that signaled the riots were over. Turning to an assistant, he said, "Ah, the bells! We're winning." "Who's 'we,' *mon prince*?" the assistant asked. Gesturing for the man to keep quiet, Talleyrand replied, "Not a word! I'll tell you who we are tomorrow." He well knew that only fools rush into a situation – that by

willing, I'll divide the cheese in two and you'll both be satisfied."
"Agreed," said the cat and the dog.
So the fox took out his knife and cut the cheese in two, but , instead of cutting it lengthwise, he cut it in the width.
"My half is smaller!" protested the dog.
The fox looked judiciously through his spectacles at the dog's share.
"You're right, quite right!" he decided.
So he went and bit off a piece of the cat's share.
"That will make it even!" he said.
When the cat saw what the fox did she began to yowl:
"Just look! My part's smaller now!"
The fox again put on his spectacles and

committing too quickly you lose your maneuverability. People also respect you less: Perhaps tomorrow, they think, you will commit to another, different cause, since you gave yourself so easily to this one. Commitment to one side deprives you of the advantage of time and the luxury of waiting. Let others fall in love with this group or that; for your part don't rush in, don't lose your head.

Image: The center of attention, desire, and worship. Never succumbing to one suitor or the other, yet encouraging them to fight amongst themselves, the Virgin Queen keeps them all revolving around her like planets, unable to leave her orbit but never getting any closer to her.

Authority: Do not commit yourself to anybody or anything, for that is to be a slave, a slave to every man. Independence is more precious than the gift in exchange for which independence is lost. You should prefer many people to depend upon you rather than that you should depend upon any single person. Above all, keep yourself free of commitments and obligations – they are the device of another to get you into his power ... (Baltasar Gracian, 1601–1658)

PLAY A SUCKER TO CATCH A SUCKER – SEEM DUMBER THAN YOUR MARK

JUDGMENT

No one likes feeling stupider than the next person. The trick, then, is to make your victims feel smart – and not just smart, but smarter than you are. Once convinced of this, they will never suspect that you may have ulterior motives.

Now, there is nothing of which a man is prouder than of intellectual ability, for it is this that gives him his commanding place in the animal world. It is an exceedingly rash thing to let anyone see that you are decidedly superior to him in this respect, and to let other people see it too ... Hence, while rank and riches may always reckon upon deferential treatment in society, that is something which intellectual ability can never expect; to be ignored is the greatest favour shown to it; and if people notice it at all, it is because they regard it as a piece of impertinence, or else as something to which its

The feeling that someone else is more intelligent than we are is almost intolerable. We usually try to justify it in different ways: "He only has book knowledge, whereas I have real knowledge." "Her parents paid for her to get a good education. If my parents had had as much money, if I had been as privileged ..." "He's not as smart as he thinks."

Given how important the idea of intelligence is to most people's vanity, it is critical never inadvertently to insult or impugn a person's brain power. That is an unforgivable sin. But if you can make this iron rule work for you, it opens up all sorts of avenues of deception. Subliminally reassure people that they are more intelligent than you are, or even that you are a bit of a moron, and you can run rings around them. The feeling of intellectual superiority you give them will disarm their suspicion-muscles.

In 1865, the Prussian councilor Otto von Bismarck wanted Austria to sign a certain treaty. The treaty was totally in the interests of Prussia and against the interests of Austria, and Bismarck would have to strategize to get the Austrians to agree to it. But the Austrian negotiator, Count Blome, was an avid card player. His particular game was quinze, and he often said that he could judge a man's character by the way he played quinze. Bismarck knew of this saying of Blome's.

The night before the negotiations were to begin, Bismarck innocently engaged Blome in a game of quinze. The Prussian would later write, "I played so recklessly that everyone was astonished. I lost several thousand talers [the currency of the time], but I succeeded in fooling [Blome], for he believed me to be more venturesome than I am and I gave way." Besides appearing reckless, Bismarck also played the witless fool, saying ridiculous things and bumbling about with a surplus of nervous energy.

All this made Blome feel he had gathered valuable information. He knew that Bismarck was aggressive – the Prussian already had that reputation, and the way he played had confirmed it. And aggressive men, Blome knew, can be foolish and rash. A heedless fool like Bismarck, he thought, is incapable of cold-blooded calculation and deception, so he only glanced at the treaty before signing it. As soon as the ink was dry, a joyous Bismarck exclaimed in his face, "Well, I could never have believed that I should find an Austrian diplomat willing to sign that document!"

The Chinese have a phrase, "Masquerading as a swine to kill the tiger." This refers to an ancient hunting technique in which the hunter clothes himself in the hide and snout of a pig, and mimics its grunting. The mighty tiger thinks a pig is coming his way, and lets it get close, savoring the prospect of an easy meal. But it is the hunter who has the last laugh.

Masquerading as a swine works wonders on those who, like tigers, are arrogant and overconfident: The easier they think it is to prey on you, the more easily you can turn the tables.

Intelligence is the obvious quality to downplay, but why stop there? Taste and sophistication rank close to intelligence on

possessor has no legitimate right, and upon which he dares to pride himself; and in retaliation and revenge for his conduct, people secretly try and humiliate him in some other way; and if they wait to do this, it is only for a fitting opportunity. A man may be as humble as possible in his demeanour, and yet hardly ever get people to overlook his crime in standing intellectually above them. In the Garden of Roses, *Sadi makes the remark: "You should know that foolish people are a hundredfold more averse to meeting the wise than the wise are indisposed for the company of the foolish."* On the other hand, it is a real recommendation*

to be stupid. For
just as warmth is
agreeable to the
body, so it does
the mind good to
feel its
superiority; and
a man will seek
company likely
to give him this
feeling, as
instinctively as
he will approach
the fireplace or
walk in the sun if
he wants to get
warm. But this
means that he
will be disliked
on account of his
superiority; and
if a man is to be
liked, he must
really be inferior
in point of
intellect.

ARTHUR
SCHOPENHAUER,
1788–1860

the vanity scale; make people feel they are more sophisticated than you are and their guard will come down. They will keep you around because you make them feel better about themselves, and the longer you are around, the more opportunities you will have to deceive them.

Image: The Opossum. In playing dead, the opossum plays stupid. Many a predator has therefore left it alone. Who could believe that such an ugly, unintelligent, nervous little creature could be capable of such deception?

Authority: Know how to make use of stupidity: the wisest man plays this card at times. There are occasions when the highest wisdom consists in appearing not to know – you must not be ignorant but capable of playing it. It is not much good being wise among fools and sane among lunatics. He who poses as a fool is not a fool. The best way to be well received by all is to clothe yourself in the skin of the dumbest of brutes. (Baltasar Gracian, 1601–1658)

USE THE SURRENDER

TACTIC: TRANSFORM

WEAKNESS INTO POWER

JUDGMENT

When you are weaker, never fight for honor's sake; choose surrender instead. Surrender gives you time to recover, time to torment and irritate your conqueror, time to wait for his power to wane. Do not give him the satisfaction of fighting and defeating you – surrender first. By turning the other cheek you infuriate and unsettle him. Make surrender a tool of power.

KEYS TO POWER

What gets us into trouble in the realm of power is often our own overreaction to the moves of our enemies and rivals. That overreaction creates problems we would have avoided had we been more reasonable. It also has an endless rebound effect, for the enemy then overreacts as well. It is always our first instinct to react, to meet aggression with some other kind of aggression. But the next time someone pushes you and you find yourself starting to react, try this: Do not resist or fight back, but yield, turn the other cheek, bend. You will find that this often neutralizes their behavior – they expected, even wanted you to react with force and so they are caught off-guard and confounded by your lack of resistance. By yielding, you in fact control the situation, because your surrender is part of a larger plan to lull them into believing they have defeated you.

This is the essence of the surrender tactic: Inwardly you stay firm, but outwardly you bend. Deprived of a reason to get angry, your opponents will often be bewildered instead. And they are unlikely to react with more violence, which would demand a reaction from you. Instead you are allowed the time and space to plot the countermoves that will bring them down. In the battle of the intelligent against the brutal and the aggressive, the surrender tactic is the supreme weapon.

In many cases it is better to surrender than to fight; faced with a more powerful opponent and a sure defeat, it is often also better to surrender than to run away. Running away may save you for the time being, but the aggressor will eventually catch up with you. If you surrender instead, you have an opportunity to coil around your enemy and strike with your fangs from close up.

In 473 B.C., in ancient China, King Goujian of Yue suffered a horrible defeat from the ruler of Wu in the battle of Fujiao. Goujian wanted to flee, but he had an adviser who told him to surrender and to place himself in the service of the ruler of Wu, from which position he could study the man and plot his revenge. Deciding to follow this advice, Goujian gave the ruler all of his riches, and went to work in his conqueror's stables as the lowest servant. For three years he humbled himself before the ruler, who then, finally satisfied of his loyalty, allowed him to return home. Inwardly, however, Goujian had spent those three years gathering information and plotting revenge. When a terrible drought struck Wu, and the kingdom was weakened by inner turmoil, he raised an army, invaded, and won with ease. That is the power behind surrender: It gives you the time and the flexibility to plot a devastating counterblow. Had Goujian run away, he would have lost this chance.

Power is always in flux – since the game is by nature fluid, and an arena of struggle, those with power almost always find themselves eventually on the downward swing. If you find yourself temporarily weakened, the surrender tactic is perfect for raising yourself up again – it disguises your ambition; it teaches you patience and self-control, key skills in the game; and it puts you in the best possible position for taking advantage of your oppressor's sudden slide. If you run

Voltaire was living in exile in London at a time when anti-French sentiment was at its highest. One day, walking through the streets, he found himself surrounded by an angry crowd. "Hang him. Hang the Frenchman," they yelled. Voltaire calmly addressed the mob with the following words: "Men of England! You wish to kill me because I am a Frenchman. Am I not punished enough in not being born an Englishman?" The crowd cheered his thoughtful words, and escorted him safely back to his lodgings.

IN CLIFTON FADIMAN, ED., THE LITTLE, BROWN BOOK OF ANECDOTES, 1985

away or fight back, in the long run you cannot win. If you surrender, you will almost always emerge victorious.

> Image: An Oak Tree. The oak that resists the wind loses its branches one by one, and with nothing left to protect it, the trunk finally snaps. The oak that bends lives longer, its trunk growing wider, its roots deeper and more tenacious.

> Authority: Ye have heard that it hath been said, An eye for an eye and a tooth for a tooth: But I say unto you, That ye resist not evil: but whosoever shall smite thee on thy right cheek, turn to him the other also. And if any man will sue thee at the law, and take away thy coat, let them have thy cloak also. And whosoever shall compel thee to go a mile, go with him twain. (Jesus Christ, in Matthew 5: 38–41)

CONCENTRATE
YOUR FORCES

JUDGMENT

*Conserve your forces and energies by keeping them con-
centrated at their strongest point. You gain more by finding a rich mine and mining it deeper than by flitting
from one shallow mine to another – intensity defeats
extensity every time. When looking for sources of power to
elevate you, find the one key patron, the fat cow who will
give you milk for a long time to come.*

KEYS TO POWER

The world is plagued by greater and greater division – within countries, political groups, families, even individuals. We are all in a state of total distraction and diffusion, hardly able to keep our minds in one direction before we are pulled in a thousand others. The modern world's level of conflict is higher than ever, and we have internalized it in our own lives.

The solution is a form of retreat inside ourselves, to the past, to more concentrated forms of thought and action. Napoleon knew the value of concentrating your forces at the enemy's weakest spot – it was the secret of his success on the battlefield. But his willpower and his mind were equally modeled on this notion. Singlemindedness of purpose, total concentration on the goal, and the use of these qualities against people less focused, people in a state of distraction – such an arrow will find its mark every time and overwhelm the enemy.

Casanova attributed his success in life to his ability to concentrate on a single goal and push at it until it yielded. It was his ability to give himself over completely to the women he desired that made him so intensely seductive. For the weeks or months that one of these women lived in his orbit, he thought of no one else. When he was imprisoned in the treacherous "leads" of the doge's palace in Venice, a prison from which no one had ever escaped, he concentrated his mind on the single goal of escape, day after day. A change of cells, which meant that months of digging had all been for naught, did not discourage him; he persisted and eventually escaped. "I have always believed," he later wrote, "that when a man gets it into his head to do something, and when he exclusively occupies himself in that design, he must succeed, whatever the difficulties. That man will become Grand Vizier or Pope."

In the world of power you will constantly need help from other people, usually those more powerful than you. The fool flits from one person to another, believing that he will survive by spreading himself out. It is a corollary of the law of concentration, however, that much energy is saved, and more power is attained, by affixing yourself to a single, appropriate souce of power. The scientist Nikolai Tesla ruined himself by believing that he somehow maintained his independence by not having to serve a single master. He even turned down J. P. Morgan, who offered him a rich contract. In the end, Tesla's "independence" meant that he could depend on no single patron, but was always having to toady up to a dozen of them. Later in his life he realized his mistake. In the end, the single patron appreciates your loyalty and becomes dependent on your services; in the long run the master serves the slave.

Finally, power itself always exists in concentrated forms. In any organization it is inevitable for a small group to hold the strings. And often it is not those with the titles. You must find out who controls the operations, who is the real director behind the scenes. As Richelieu discovered at the beginning of his rise to the top of the French political scene during the early seventeenth century, it was not King Louis XIII who decided things, it was the king's mother. And

Beware of dissipating your powers; strive constantly to concentrate them. Genius thinks it can do whatever it sees others doing, but it is sure to repent of every ill-judged outlay.

JOHANN GOETHE, 1749–1832

so he attached himself to her, and catapulted through the ranks of the courtiers, all the way to the top.

It is enough to strike oil once – your wealth and power are assured for a lifetime.

Image: The Arrow. You cannot hit two targets with one arrow. If your thoughts stray, you miss the enemy's heart. Mind and arrow must become one. Only with such concentration of mental and physical power can your arrow hit the tar-get and pierce the heart.

Authority: Prize intensity more than extensity. Perfection resides in quality, not quantity. Extent alone never rises above mediocrity, and it is the misfortune of men with wide general interests that while they would like to have their finger in every pie, they have one in none. Intensity gives eminence, and rises to the heroic in matters sublime. (Baltasar Gracian, 1601–1658)

PLAY THE PERFECT

COURTIER

JUDGMENT

The perfect courtier thrives in a world where everything revolves around power and political dexterity. He has mastered the art of indirection; he flatters, yields to superiors, and asserts power over others in the most oblique and graceful manner. Learn and apply the laws of courtiership and there will be no limit to how far you can rise in the court.

Avoid ostentation. It is never prudent to prattle on about yourself or call too much attention to your actions. The more you talk about your deeds the more suspicion you cause. You also stir up enough envy among your peers to induce treachery and backstabbing.

Practice nonchalance. Never seem to be working too hard. Your talent must appear to flow naturally, with an ease that makes people take you for a genius rather than a workaholic. It is better for them to marvel at how gracefully you have achieved your accomplishment than to wonder why it took so much work.

Be frugal with flattery. It may seem that your superiors cannot get enough flattery, but too much of even a good thing loses its value. Learn to flatter indirectly – by downplaying your own contribution, for example, to make your master look better.

Arrange to be noticed. There is a paradox: You cannot display yourself too brazenly, yet you must also get yourself noticed. You stand no chance of rising if the ruler does not notice you in the swamp of courtiers. This task requires much art. It is often initially a matter of being seen, in the literal sense. Pay attention to your physical appearance, then, and find a way to create a distinctive – a *subtly* distinctive – style and image.

Alter your style and language according to the person you are dealing with. The pseudo-belief in equality – the idea that talking and acting the same way with everyone, no matter what their rank, makes you somehow a paragon of civilization – is a terrible mistake. Those below you will take it as a form of condescension, which it is, and those above you will be offended, although they may not admit it. You must change your style and your way of speaking to suit each person. This is not lying, it is acting, and acting is an art, not a gift from God.

Never be the bearer of bad news. The king kills the messenger who brings bad news: this is a cliché, but there is truth to it. You must struggle and if necessary lie and cheat to be sure that the lot of the bearer of bad news falls on a colleague, never on you.

Never affect friendliness and intimacy with your master. He does not want a friend for a subordinate, he wants a subordinate. Never approach him in an easy, friendly way, or act as if you are on the best of terms – that is *his* prerogative.

Never criticize those above you directly. This may seem obvious, but there are often times when some sort of criticism is necessary – to say nothing, or to give no advice, would open you to risks of another sort. You must learn, however, to couch your advice and criticism as indirectly and as politely as possible.

Be frugal in asking those above you for favors. Nothing irritates a master more than having to reject someone's request. It stirs up

It is a wise thing to be polite; consequently, it is a stupid thing to be rude. To make enemies by unnecessary and wilful incivility is just as insane a proceeding as to set your house on fire. For politeness is like a counter – an avowedly false coin, with which it is foolish to be stingy. A sensible man will be generous in the use of it ... Wax, a substance naturally hard and brittle, can be made soft by the application of a little warmth, so that it will take any shape you please. In the same way, by being polite and friendly, you can make people pliable and obliging, even though they are apt to be crabbed and malevolent. Hence politeness is to human

nature what warmth is to wax.

ARTHUR SCHOPENHAUER, 1788–1860

guilt and resentment. Ask for favors as rarely as possible, and know when to stop. Most important: Do not ask for favors on another person's behalf, least of all a friend's.

Never joke about appearances or taste. A lively wit and a humorous disposition are essential qualities for a good courtier, and there are times when vulgarity is appropriate and engaging. But avoid any kind of joke about appearance or taste, two highly sensitive areas, especially with those above you.

Do not be the court cynic. Express admiration for the good work of others. If you constantly criticize your equals or subordinates some of that criticism will rub off on you, hovering over you like a gray cloud wherever you go. People will groan at each new cynical comment, and you will irritate them. By expressing modest admiration for other people's achievements, you paradoxically call attention to your own.

Be self-observant. The mirror is a miraculous invention; without it you would commit great sins against beauty and decorum. You also need a mirror for your actions. This can sometimes come from other people telling you what they see in you, but that is not the most trustworthy method: *You* must be the mirror, training your mind to try to see yourself as others see you. Are you acting too obsequious? Are you trying too hard to please? Be observant about yourself and you will avoid a mountain of blunders.

Master your emotions. As an actor in a

great play, you must learn to cry and laugh on command and when it is appropriate. You must be able both to disguise your anger and frustration and to fake your contentment and agreement. You must be the master of your own face.

Fit the spirit of the times. A slight affectation of a past era can be charming, as long as you choose a period at least twenty years back; wearing the fashions of ten years ago is ludicrous, unless you enjoy the role of court jester. Your spirit and way of thinking must keep up with the times, even if the times offend your sensibilities. Be too forward-thinking, however, and no one will understand you.

Be a source of pleasure. This is critical. It is an obvious law of human nature that we will flee what is unpleasant and distasteful, while charm and the promise of delight will draw us like moths to a flame. There are degrees to this: Not everyone can play the role of favorite, for not everyone is blessed with charm and wit. But we can all control our unpleasant qualities and obscure them when necessary.

RE-CREATE YOURSELF

JUDGMENT

Do not accept the roles that society foists on you. Re-create yourself by forging a new identity, one that commands attention and never bores the audience. Be the master of your own image rather than letting others define it for you. Incorporate dramatic devices into your public gestures and actions – your power will be enhanced and your character will seem larger than life.

KEYS TO POWER

The character you seem to have been born with is not necessarily who you are; beyond the characteristics you have inherited, your parents, your friends, and your peers have helped to shape your personality. The Promethean task of the powerful is to take control of the process, to stop allowing others that ability to limit and mold them. Remake yourself into a character of power. Working on yourself like clay should be one of your greatest and most pleasurable life tasks. It makes you in essence an artist – an artist creating yourself.

The first step in the process of self-creation is self-consciousness – being aware of yourself as an actor and taking control of your appearance and emotions. As Diderot said, the bad actor is the one who is always sincere. People who wear their hearts on their sleeves out in society are tiresome and embarrassing. Their sincerity notwithstanding, it is hard to take them seriously. Those who cry in public may temporarily elicit sympathy, but sympathy soon turns to scorn and irritation at their self-obsessiveness.

Good actors control themselves better. They can play sincere and heartfelt, can affect a tear and a compassionate look at will, but they don't have to feel it. They externalize emotion in a form that others can understand. Method acting is fatal in the real world. No ruler or leader could possibly play the part if all of the emotions he showed had to be real. So learn self-control. Adopt the plasticity of the actor, who can mold his or her face to the emotion required.

The second step in the process of self-

The man who intends to make his fortune in this ancient capital of the world [Rome] must be a chameleon susceptible of reflecting the colors of the atmosphere that surrounds him – a Proteus apt to assume every form, every shape. He must be supple, flexible, insinuating, close, inscrutable, often base, sometimes sincere, sometimes perfidious, always concealing a part of his knowledge, indulging in but one tone of voice, patient, a perfect master of his own countenance, as cold as ice when any other man would be all fire; and if unfortunately he is not religious at heart – a very

creation is the creation of a memorable character, one that compels attention, that stands out above the other players on the stage. This was the game Abraham Lincoln played. The homespun, common country man, he knew, was a kind of president that America had never had but would delight in electing. Although many of these qualities came naturally to him, he played them up – the hat and clothes, the beard. (No president before him had worn a beard.)

Good drama, however, needs more than an interesting appearance, or a single stand-out moment. Drama takes place over time – it is an unfolding event. Rhythm and timing are critical. One of the most important elements in the rhythm of drama is suspense. The key to keeping the audience on the edge of their seats is letting events unfold slowly, then speeding them up at the right moment, according to a pattern and tempo that you control. Great rulers from Napoleon to Mao Tse-tung have used theatrical timing to surprise and divert their public.

Remember that overacting can be counterproductive – it is another way of spending too much effort trying to attract attention. The actor Richard Burton discovered early in his career that by standing totally still onstage, he drew attention to himself and away from the other actors. It is less what you do that matters, clearly, than how you do it – your gracefulness and imposing stillness on the social stage count for more than overdoing your part and moving around too much.

Finally: Learn to play many roles, to be whatever the moment requires. Adapt your mask to the situation – be protean in the faces you wear. Bismarck played this game to perfection: to a liberal he was a liberal, to a hawk he was a hawk. He could not be grasped, and what cannot be grasped cannot be consumed.

Image: The Greek Sea-God Proteus. His power came from his ability to change shape at will, to be whatever the moment required. When Menelaus, brother of Agamemnon, tried to seize him, Proteus transformed himself into a lion, then a serpent, a panther, a boar, running water, and finally a leafy tree.

Authority: Know how to be all things to all men. A discreet Proteus – a scholar among scholars, a saint among saints. That is the art of winning over everyone, for like attracts like. Take note of temperaments and adapt yourself to that of each person you meet – follow the lead of the serious and jovial in turn, changing your mood discreetly. (Baltasar Gracian, 1601–1658)

KEEP YOUR HANDS

CLEAN

JUDGMENT

You must seem a paragon of efficiency and civility: your hands are never soiled by mistakes and nasty deeds. Maintain such a spotless appearance by using others as unwitting pawns and screens to disguise your involvement.

KEYS TO POWER

Occasional mistakes are inevitable – the world is just too unpredictable. People of power, however, are undone not by the mistakes they make, but by the way they deal with them. Like surgeons, they must cut away the tumor with speed and finality. Excuses and apologies are much too blunt tools for this delicate operation; the powerful avoid them. By apologizing you open up all sorts of doubts about your competence, your intentions, any other mistakes you may not have confessed. Excuses satisfy no one and apologies make everyone uncomfortable. The mistake does not vanish with an apology; it deepens and festers. Better to cut it off instantly, distract attention from yourself, and focus attention on a convenient scapegoat before people have time to ponder your responsibility or your possible incompetence.

It is often wise to choose the most innocent victim possible as a sacrificial goat. Such people will not be powerful enough to fight you, and their naive protests may be seen as protesting too much – may be seen, in other words, as a sign of their guilt. Be careful, however, not to create a martyr. It is important that *you* remain the victim, the poor leader betrayed by the incompetence of those around you. If the scapegoat appears too weak and his punishment too cruel, you may end up the victim of your own device. Sometimes you should find a more powerful scapegoat – one who will elicit less sympathy in the long run.

In this vein history has time and again shown the value of using a close associate as

Do everything pleasant yourself, everything unpleasant through third parties. By adopting the first course you win favor, by taking the second you deflect ill will. Important affairs often require rewards and punishments. Let only the good come from you and the evil from others.

BALTASAR GRACIAN, 1601–1658

a scapegoat. This is known as the "fall of the favorite."

As a leader you must never dirty your hands with ugly tasks or bloody deeds, anything that will make you look ugly and abusive of your high position. Yet power cannot survive without the constant squashing of enemies – there will always be dirty little tasks that have to be done to keep you in power. What is required is a cat's-paw, someone who does the dirty, dangerous work for you. Similar to the scapegoat, the cat's-paw will help you preserve your spotless reputation.

The cat's-paw will usually be a person from outside your immediate circle, who will therefore be unlikely to realize how he or she is being used. You will find these dupes everywhere – people who enjoy doing you favors, especially if you throw them a minimal bone or two in exchange. But as they accomplish tasks that may seem to them innocent enough, or at least completely justified, they are actually clearing the field for you, spreading the information you feed them, undermining people they do not realize are your rivals, inadvertently furthering your cause, dirtying their hands while yours remain clean.

The easiest and most effective way to use a cat's-paw is often to plant information with him that he will then spread to your primary target. False or planted information is a powerful tool, especially if spread by a dupe whom no one suspects. You will find it very easy to play innocent and disguise yourself as the source.

In any event, you must always get someone else to be the executioner, or the bearer of bad news, while you bring only joy and glad tidings.

Image: The Innocent Goat. On the Day of Atonement, the high priest brings the goat into the temple, places his hands on its head, and confesses the people's sins, transferring guilt to the guiltless beast, which is then led to the wilderness and abandoned, the people's sins and blame vanishing with him.

Authority: Folly consists not in committing Folly, but in being incapable of concealing it. All men make mistakes, but the wise conceal the blunders they have made, while fools make them public. Reputation depends more on what is hidden than on what is seen. If you can't be good, be careful. (Baltasar Gracian, 1601–1658)

PLAY ON PEOPLE'S NEED TO BELIEVE TO CREATE A CULTLIKE FOLLOWING

JUDGMENT

People have an overwhelming desire to believe in something. Become the focal point of such desire by offering them a cause, a new faith to follow. Keep your words vague but full of promise; emphasize enthusiasm over rationality and clear thinking. Give your new disciples rituals to perform, ask them to make sacrifices on your behalf. In the absence of organized religion and grand causes, your new belief system will bring you untold power.

HOW TO CREATE A CULT IN FIVE EASY STEPS

In searching, as you must, for the methods that will gain you the most power for the least effort, you will find the creation of a cultlike following one of the most effective. Having a large following opens up all sorts of possibilities for deception; not only will your followers worship you, they will defend you from your enemies and will voluntarily take on the work of enticing others to join your fledgling cult. This kind of power will lift you to another realm: you will no longer have to struggle or use subterfuge to enforce your will. You are adored and can do no wrong.

You might think it a gargantuan task to create such a following, but in fact it is fairly simple. Always in a rush to believe in something, people will manufacture saints and faiths out of nothing. Do not let this gullibility go to waste: make yourself the object of worship. Make people form a cult around you by following these five easy steps.

Step 1: Keep It Vague, Keep It Simple.

To create a cult you must first attract attention. This you should do not through actions, which are too clear and readable, but through words, which are hazy and deceptive. Your initial speeches, conversations, and interviews must include two elements: on the one hand the promise of something great and transformative, and on the other a total vagueness. This combination will stimulate all kinds of hazy dreams in your listeners, who will make their own connections and see what they want to see.

Try to make the subject of your cult new

To become the founder of a new religion one must be psychologically infallible in one's knowledge of a certain average type of souls who have not yet recognized that they belong together.

FRIEDRICH NIETZSCHE, 1844–1900

and fresh, so that few will understand it. Done right, the combination of vague promises, cloudy but alluring concepts, and fiery enthusiasm will stir people's souls and a group will form around you.

Step 2: Emphasize the Visual and the Sensual over the Intellectual. Once people have begun to gather around you, two dangers will present themselves: boredom and skepticism. Boredom will make people go elsewhere; skepticism will allow them the distance to think rationally about whatever it is you are offering, blowing away the mist you have artfully created and revealing your ideas for what they are. You need to amuse the bored, then, and ward off the cynics.

The best way to do this is through theater, or other devices of its kind. Surround yourself with luxury, dazzle your followers with visual splendor, fill their eyes with spectacle. Not only will this keep them from seeing the ridiculousness of your ideas, the holes in your belief system, it will also attract more attention, more followers.

Step 3: Borrow the Forms of Organized Religion to Structure the Group. Your cultlike following is growing; it is time to organize it. Find a way both elevating and comforting. Organized religions have long held unquestioned authority for large numbers of people, and continue to do so in our supposedly secular age. Create rituals for your followers; organize them into a hierarchy, giving them titles that resound with religious overtones; ask them for sacrifices that will fill your coffers and increase your power.

Step 4: Disguise Your Source of Income.
Your group has grown, and you have structured it in a churchlike form. Your coffers are beginning to fill with your followers' money. Yet you must never be seen as hungry for money and the power it brings. It is at this moment that you must disguise the source of your income.

Your followers want to believe that if they follow you all sorts of good things will fall into their lap. By surrounding yourself with luxury you become living proof of the soundness of your belief system. Never reveal that your wealth actually comes from your followers' pockets; instead, make it seem to come from the truth of your methods.

It was to the charlatan's advantage that the individuals predisposed to credulity should multiply, that the groups of his adherents should enlarge to mass proportions, guaranteeing an ever greater scope for his triumphs.

THE POWER OF THE CHARLATAN, GRETE DE FRANCESCO, 1939

Step 5: Set Up an Us-versus-Them Dynamic. The group is now large and thriving, a magnet attracting more and more particles. If you are not careful, though, inertia will set in, and time and boredom will demagnetize the group. To keep your followers united, you must now do what all religions and belief systems have done: create an us-versus-them dynamic.

First, make sure your followers believe they are part of an exclusive club, unified by a bond of common goals. Then, to strengthen this bond, manufacture the notion of a devious enemy out to ruin you. If you have no enemies, invent one.

LAW
28

ENTER ACTION
WITH BOLDNESS

JUDGMENT

If you are unsure of a course of action, do not attempt it. Your doubts and hesitations will infect your execution. Timidity is dangerous: better to enter with boldness. Any mistakes you commit through audacity are easily corrected with more audacity. Everyone admires the bold; no one honors the timid.

KEYS TO POWER

Most of us are timid. We want to avoid tension and conflict and we want to be liked by all. We may contemplate a bold action but we rarely bring it to life. We are terrified of the consequences, of what others might think of us, of the hostility we will stir up if we dare go beyond our usual place.

Although we may disguise our timidity as a concern for others, a desire not to hurt or offend them, in fact it is the opposite – we are really self-absorbed, worried about ourselves and how others perceive us. Boldness, on the other hand, is outer-directed, and often makes people feel more at ease, since it is less self-conscious and less repressed. It never induces awkwardness or embarrassment. And so we admire the bold, and prefer to be around them, because their self-confidence infects us and draws us outside our own realm of inwardness and reflection.

Few are born bold. Even Napoleon had to cultivate the habit on the battlefield, where he knew it was a matter of life and death. In social settings he was awkward and timid, but he overcame this and practiced boldness in every part of his life because he saw its tremendous power, how it could literally enlarge a man (even one who, like Napoleon, was in fact conspicuously small).

You must practice and develop your boldness. You will often find uses for it. The best place to begin is often the delicate world of negotiation, particularly those discussions in which you are asked to set your own price. How often we put ourselves down by asking for too little. When Christopher Columbus proposed that the Spanish court finance his

HOW TO BE VICTORIOUS IN LOVE

But with those who have made an impression upon your heart, I have noticed that you are timid. This quality might affect a bourgeoise, but you must attack the heart of a woman of the world with other weapons ... I tell you on behalf of women: there is not one of us who does not prefer a little rough handling to too much consideration. Men lose through blundering more hearts than virtue saves. The more timidity a lover shows with us the more it concerns our pride to goad him on; the more respect he has for our resistance, the more respect we demand of him. We would

voyage to the Americas, he also made the insanely bold demand that he be called "Grand Admiral of the Ocean." The court agreed. The price he set was the price he received – he demanded to be treated with respect, and so he was. Henry Kissinger too knew that in negotiation bold demands work better than starting off with piecemeal concessions and trying to meet the other person halfway. Set your value high, and then, set it higher.

People have a sixth sense for the weaknesses of others. If, in a first encounter, you demonstrate your willingness to compromise, back down, and retreat, you bring out the lion even in people who are not necessarily bloodthirsty. Everything depends on perception, and once you are seen as the kind of person who quickly goes on the defensive, who is willing to negotiate and be amenable, you will be pushed around without mercy. It is always best, then, to create an impression with your first appearance, to enter action with boldness.

A bold move makes you seem larger and more powerful than you are. If it comes suddenly, with the stealth and swiftness of a snake, it inspires that much more fear. By intimidating with a bold move, you establish a precedent: in every subsequent encounter, people will be on the defensive, in terror of your next strike.

cannot act like an idiot.

LIFE, LETTERS, AND EPICUREAN PHILOSOPHY OF NINON DE L'ENCLOS, NINON DE L'ENCLOS, 1623–1706

Image: The Lion creates no gaps in his way – his movements are too swift, his jaws too quick and powerful. The timid hare will do anything to escape danger, but in its haste to retreat and flee, it backs into traps, hops smack into its enemies' jaws.

Authority: I certainly think that it is better to be impetuous than cautious, for fortune is a woman, and it is necessary, if you wish to master her, to conquer her by force; and it can be seen that she lets herself be overcome by the bold rather than by those who proceed coldly. And therefore, like a woman, she is always a friend to the young, because they are less cautious, fiercer, and master her with greater audacity. (Niccolò Machiavelli, 1469–1527)

PLAN ALL THE WAY
TO THE END

JUDGMENT

The ending is everything. Plan all the way to it, taking into account all the possible consequences, obstacles, and twists of fortune that might reverse your hard work and give the glory to others. By planning to the end you will not be overwhelmed by circumstances and you will know when to stop. Gently guide fortune and help determine the future by thinking far ahead.

KEYS TO POWER

According to the cosmology of the ancient Greeks, the gods were thought to have complete vision into the future. They saw everything to come, right down to the intricate details. Men, on the other hand, were seen as victims of fate, trapped in the moment and their emotions, unable to see beyond immediate dangers. Those heroes, such as Odysseus, who were able to look beyond the present and plan several steps ahead seemed to defy fate, to approximate the gods in their ability to determine the future. The comparison is still valid – those among us who think farther ahead and patiently bring their plans to fruition seem to have a godlike power.

Because most people are too imprisoned in the moment to plan with this kind of foresight, the ability to ignore immediate dangers and pleasures translates into power. It is the power of being able to overcome the natural human tendency to react to things as they happen, and instead to train oneself to step back, imagining the larger things taking shape beyond one's immediate vision.

In 415 B.C., the ancient Athenians attacked Sicily, believing their expedition would bring them riches, power, and a glorious ending to the sixteen-year Peloponnesian War. They did not consider the dangers of an invasion so far from home; they did not foresee that the Sicilians would fight all the harder since the battles were on their own homeland, or that all of Athens' enemies would band together against them, or that war would break out on several fronts, stretching their forces way too thin.

Two frogs dwelt in the same pool. The pool being dried up under the summer's heat, they left it, and set out together to seek another home. As they went along they chanced to pass a deep well, amply supplied with water, on seeing which one of the frogs said to the other: "Let us descend and make our abode in this well, it will furnish us with shelter and food." The other replied with greater caution: "But suppose the water should fail us, how can we get out again from so great a depth?" Do nothing without a regard to the consequences.

FABLES, AESOP, LATE SIXTH CENTURY B.C.

The Sicilian expedition was a complete disaster, leading to the destruction of one of the greatest civilizations of all time. The Athenians were led into this disaster by their hearts, not their minds. They saw only the chance of glory, not the dangers that loomed in the distance.

According to Cardinal de Retz, "The most ordinary cause of people's mistakes is their being too much frightened at the present danger, and not enough so at that which is remote." The dangers that are remote, that loom in the distance – if we can see them as they take shape, how many mistakes we avoid. How many plans we would instantly abort if we realized we were avoiding a small danger only to step into a larger one. So much of power is not what you do but what you do not do – the rash and foolish actions that you refrain from before they get you into trouble. Plan in detail before you act – do not let vague plans lead you into trouble. Will this have unintended consequences? Will I stir up new enemies? Will someone else take advantage of my labors? Unhappy endings are much more common than happy ones – do not be swayed by the happy ending in your mind.

When you see several steps ahead, and plan your moves all the way to the end, you will no longer be tempted by emotion or by the desire to improvise. Your clarity will rid you of the anxiety and vagueness that are the primary reasons why so many fail to conclude their actions successfully. You see the ending and you tolerate no deviation.

Image: The Gods on Mount Olympus. Looking down on human actions from the clouds, they see in advance the endings of all the great dreams that lead to disaster and tragedy. And they laugh at our inability to see beyond the moment, and at how we delude ourselves.

Authority: How much easier it is never to get in than to get yourself out! We should act contrary to the reed which, when it first appears, throws up a long straight stem but afterwards, as though it were exhausted ... makes several dense knots, indicating that it no longer has its original vigor and drive. We must rather begin gently and coolly, saving our breath for the encounter and our vigorous thrusts for finishing off the job. In their beginnings it is we who guide affairs and hold them in our power; but so often once they are set in motion, it is they which guide us and sweep us along. (Montaigne, 1533–1592)

30

MAKE YOUR
ACCOMPLISHMENTS
SEEM EFFORTLESS

JUDGMENT

Your actions must seem natural and executed with ease. All the toil and practice that go into them, and also all the clever tricks, must be concealed. When you act, act effortlessly, as if you could do much more. Avoid the temptation of revealing how hard you work — it only raises questions. Teach no one your tricks or they will be used against you.

KEYS TO POWER

Humanity's first notions of power came from primitive encounters with nature – the flash of lightning in the sky, a sudden flood, the speed and ferocity of a wild animal. These forces required no thinking, no planning – they awed us by their sudden appearance, their gracefulness, and their power over life and death. And this remains the kind of power we have always wanted to imitate. Through science and technology we have re-created the speed and sublime power of nature, but something is missing: our machines are noisy and jerky, they reveal their effort. Even the very best creations of technology cannot root out our admiration for things that move easily and effortlessly. The power of children to bend us to their will comes from a kind of seductive charm that we feel in the presence of a creature less reflective and more graceful than we are. We cannot return to such a state, but if we can create the appearance of this kind of ease, we elicit in others the kind of primitive awe that nature has always evoked in humankind.

One of the first European writers to expound this principle came from that most unnatural of environments, the Renaissance court. In *The Book of the Courtier*, published in 1528, Baldassare Castiglione describes the highly elaborate and codified manners of the perfect court citizen. And yet, Castiglione explains, the courtier must execute these gestures with what he calls *sprezzatura*, the capacity to make the difficult seem easy. He urges the courtier to "practice in all things a certain nonchalance which conceals all artistry and makes whatever one says or does

A line [of poetry] will take us hours maybe; Yet if it does not seem a moment's thought, Our stitching and unstitching has been naught.

ADAM'S CURSE, WILLIAM BUTLER YEATS, 1865–1939

seem uncontrived and effortless." We all admire the achievement of some unusual feat, but if it is accomplished naturally and gracefully, our admiration increases tenfold.

The idea of *sprezzatura* is relevant to all forms of power, for power depends vitally on appearances and the illusions you create. Your public actions are like artworks: they must have visual appeal, must create anticipation, even entertain. When you reveal the inner workings of your creation, you become just one more mortal among others. What is understandable is not awe-inspiring – we tell ourselves we could do as well if we had the money and time. Avoid the temptation of showing how clever you are – it is far more clever to conceal the mechanisms of your cleverness.

There is another reason for concealing your shortcuts and tricks: when you let this information out, you give people ideas they can use against you. You lose the advantages of keeping silent. We tend to want the world to know what we have done – we want our vanity gratified by having our hard work and cleverness applauded, we may even want sympathy for the hours it has taken to reach our point of artistry. Learn to control this propensity to blab, for its effect is often the opposite of what you expected. Remember: The more mystery surrounds your actions, the more awesome your power seems. You appear to be the only one who can do what you do – and the appearance of having an exclusive gift is immensely powerful. Finally, because you achieve your accomplishments with grace and ease, people believe that you could always do more if you tried harder.

This elicits not only admiration but a touch of fear. Your powers are untapped – no one can fathom their limits.

Image: The Racehorse. From up close we would see the strain, the effort to control the horse, the labored, painful breathing. But from the distance where we sit and watch, it is all gracefulness, flying through the air. Keep others at a distance and they will only see the ease with which you move.

Authority: For whatever action [nonchalance] accompanies, no matter how trivial it is, it not only reveals the skill of the person doing it but also very often causes it to be considered far greater than it really is. This is because it makes the onlookers believe that a man who performs well with so much facility must possess even greater skill than he does. (Baldassare Castiglione, 1478–1529)

LAW

31

CONTROL THE OPTIONS:
GET OTHERS TO PLAY
WITH THE CARDS
YOU DEAL

JUDGMENT

The best deceptions are the ones that seem to give the other person a choice: your victims feel they are in control, but are actually your puppets. Give people options that come out in your favor whichever one they choose. Force them to make choices between the lesser of two evils, both of which serve your purpose. Put them on the horns of a dilemma: they are gored wherever they turn.

KEYS TO POWER

Words like "freedom," "options," and "choice" evoke a power of possibility far beyond the reality of the benefits they entail. When examined closely, the choices we have – in the marketplace, in elections, in our jobs – tend to have noticeable limitations: they are often a matter of a choice simply between A and B, with the rest of the alphabet out of the picture. Yet as long as the faintest mirage of choice flickers on, we rarely focus on the missing options.

This supplies the clever and cunning with enormous opportunities for deception. For people who are choosing between alternatives find it hard to believe they are being manipulated or deceived; they cannot see that you are allowing them a small amount of free will in exchange for a much more powerful imposition of your own will. Setting up a narrow range of choices, then, should always be a part of your deceptions.

The following are among the most common forms of "controlling the options":

Color the Choices. This was a favored technique of Henry Kissinger. As President Richard Nixon's secretary of state, Kissinger considered himself better informed than his boss. But if he tried to determine policy, he would offend or perhaps enrage a notoriously insecure man. So Kissinger would propose three or four choices of action for each situation, and would present them in such a way that the one he preferred always seemed the best solution compared to the others. Time after time, Nixon fell for the bait, never suspecting that he was moving where

J. P. Morgan Sr once told a jeweler of his acquaintance that he was interested in buying a pearl scarf-pin. Just a few weeks later, the jeweler happened upon a magnificent pearl. He had it mounted in an appropriate setting and sent it to Morgan, together with a bill for $5,000. The following day the package was returned. Morgan's accompanying note read: "I like the pin, but I don't like the price. If you will accept the enclosed check for $4,000, please send back the box with the seal unbroken." The enraged jeweler refused the check and dismissed the messenger in disgust. He opened up the box to reclaim the unwanted *pin, only to find that it had been removed. In its place was a check for $5,000.*

QUOTED IN
CLIFTON
FADIMAN, ED.,
THE LITTLE,
BROWN BOOK OF
ANECDOTES,
1985

Kissinger pushed him.

Force the Resister. This is a good technique to use on children and other willful people who enjoy doing the opposite of what you ask them to: Push them to "choose" what you want them to do by appearing to advocate the opposite.

Alter the Playing Field. In the 1860s, John D. Rockefeller set out to create an oil monopoly. If he tried to buy up the smaller oil companies they would figure out what he was doing and fight back. Instead, he began secretly buying up the railway companies that transported the oil. Rockefeller altered the playing field so that the only options the small oil-producers had were the ones he gave them.

The Shrinking Options. Raise your price every time the buyer hesitates and another day goes by. This is an excellent negotiating ploy to use on the chronically indecisive, who will fall for the idea that they are getting a better deal today than if they wait till tomorrow.

The Weak Man on the Precipice. This tactic is similar to "Color the Choices," but with the weak and indecisive you have to be more aggressive. Work on their emotions – use fear and terror to propel them into action. Try reason and they will always find a way to procrastinate.

Describe all sorts of dangers, exaggerating them as much as possible, until they see a yawning abyss in every direction except

The German Chancellor Bismarck, enraged at the constant criticisms from Rudolf Virchow (the German

one: the one you are pushing them to take.

The Horns of a Dilemma. This is a classic trial lawyers' technique: the lawyer leads the witnesses to decide between two possible explanations of an event, both of which poke a hole in their story. They have to answer the lawyer's questions, but whatever they say they hurt themselves. The key to this move is to strike quickly: deny the victim the time to think of an escape. As they wriggle between the horns of the dilemma, they dig their own grave.

Image: The Horns of the Bull. The bull backs you into the corner with its horns – not a single horn, which you might be able to escape, but a pair of horns that trap you within their hold. Run right or run left – either way you move into their piercing ends and are gored.

Authority: For the wounds and every other evil that men inflict upon themselves spontaneously, and of their own choice, are in the long run less painful than those inflicted by others. (Niccolò Machiavelli, 1469–1527)

pathologist and liberal politician), had his seconds call upon the scientist to challenge him to a duel. "As the challenged party, I have the choice of weapons," said Virchow, "and I choose these." He held aloft two large and apparently identical sausages. "One of these," he went on, "is infected with deadly germs; the other is perfectly sound. Let His Excellency decide which one he wishes to eat, and I will eat the other." Almost immediately the message came back that the chancellor had decided to cancel the duel.

QUOTED IN CLIFTON FADIMAN, ED., THE LITTLE, BROWN BOOK OF ANECDOTES, 1985

PLAY TO PEOPLE'S

FANTASIES

JUDGMENT

The truth is often avoided because it is ugly and unpleasant. Never appeal to truth and reality unless you are prepared for the anger that comes from disenchantment. Life is so harsh and distressing that people who can manufacture romance or conjure up fantasy are like oases in the desert: everyone flocks to them. There is great power in tapping into the fantasies of the masses.

KEYS TO POWER

Fantasy can never operate alone. It requires the backdrop of the humdrum and the mundane. It is the oppressiveness of reality that allows fantasy to take root and bloom.

The person who can spin a fantasy out of an oppressive reality has access to untold power. As you search for the fantasy that will take hold of the masses, then, keep your eye on the banal truths that weigh heavily on us all. Never be distracted by people's glamorous portraits of themselves and their lives; search and dig for what really imprisons them. Once you find that, you have the magical key that will put great power in your hands.

Although times and people change, let us examine a few of the oppressive realities that endure, and the opportunities for power they provide:

The Reality: Change is slow and gradual. It requires hard work, a bit of luck, a fair amount of self-sacrifice, and a lot of patience.
The Fantasy: A sudden transformation will bring a total change in one's fortunes, bypassing work, luck, self-sacrifice, and time in one fantastic stroke.

This is of course the fantasy par excellence of the charlatans who prowl among us to this day. Promise a great and total change – from poor to rich, sickness to health, misery to ecstasy – and you will have followers.

The Reality: The social realm has hard-set codes and boundaries. We understand these limits and know that we have to move within the same familiar circles, day in and day out.

The Fantasy: We can enter a totally new world with different codes and the promise of adventure.

In the early 1700s, all London was abuzz with talk of a mysterious stranger, a young man named George Psalmanazar. He had arrived from what was to most Englishmen a fantastical land: the island of Formosa (now Taiwan), off the coast of China. Oxford University engaged Psalmanazar to teach the island's language; a few years later he wrote a book – an immediate bestseller – on Formosa's history and geography. English royalty wined and dined the young man, and everywhere he went he entertained his hosts with wondrous stories of his homeland.

After Psalmanazar died, however, his will revealed that he was in fact merely a Frenchman with a rich imagination. Everything he had said about Formosa he had invented. He had concocted an elaborate story that fulfilled the English public's desire for the exotic and strange. British culture's rigid control of people's dangerous dreams gave him the perfect opportunity to exploit their fantasy.

The Reality: Death. The dead cannot be brought back, the past cannot be changed.
The Fantasy: A sudden reversal of this intolerable fact.

The beauty and importance of the art of Vermeer have long been recognized, but his paintings are small in number, and are extremely rare. In the 1930s, though, Vermeers began to appear on the art market. Experts were called on to verify them, and pronounced them real. It was like the resurrection of Lazurus: in a strange way, Vermeer had been brought back to life. The past had been changed.

Only later did it come out that the new Vermeers were the work of a middle-aged Dutch forger named Hans van Meegeren. And he had chosen Vermeer for his scam because he understood fantasy: The paintings would seem real precisely because the public, and the experts as well, so desperately wanted to believe they were.

Remember: the key to fantasy is distance. The distant has allure and promise, seems simple and problem free. What you are offering, then, should be ungraspable. Never let it become oppressively familiar; it is the mirage in the distance, withdrawing as the sucker approaches. As a forger of fantasies, let your victim come close enough to see and be tempted, but keep him far away enough that he stays dreaming and desiring.

Image: The Moon. Unattainable, always changing shape, disappearing and reappearing. We look at it, imagine, wonder, and pine – never familiar, continuous provoker of dreams. Do not offer the obvious. Promise the moon.

Authority: A lie is an allurement, a fabrication, that can be embellished into a fantasy. It can be clothed in the raiments of a mystic conception. Truth is cold, sober fact, not so comfortable to absorb. A lie is more palatable. The most detested person in the world is the one who always tells the truth, who never romances ... I found it far more interesting and profitable to romance than to tell the truth. (Joseph Weil, a.k.a The Yellow Kid, ˉ 1877–1976)

DISCOVER EACH

MAN'S THUMBSCREW

JUDGMENT

Everyone has a weakness, a gap in the castle wall. That weakness is usually an insecurity, an uncontrollable emotion or need; it can also be a small secret pleasure. Either way, once found, it is a thumbscrew you can turn to your advantage.

FINDING THE THUMBSCREW:
A Strategic Plan of Action

We all have resistances. We live with a perpetual armor around ourselves to defend against change and the intrusive actions of friends and rivals. One of the most important things to realize about people, though, is that they all have a weakness, some part of their psychological armor that will not resist, that will bend to your will if you find it and push on it. Some people wear their weaknesses openly, others disguise them. Those who disguise them are often the ones most effectively undone through that one chink in their armor.

In planning your assault, keep these principles in mind:

Pay Attention to Gestures and Unconscious Signals. As Sigmund Freud remarked, "No mortal can keep a secret. If his lips are silent, he chatters with his fingertips; betrayal oozes out of him at every pore." This is a critical concept in the search for a person's weakness – it is revealed by seemingly unimportant gestures and passing words.

The key is not only what you look for but where and how you look. Everyday conversation supplies the richest mine of weaknesses, so train yourself to listen.

If you suspect that someone has a particular soft spot, probe for it indirectly. Train your eye for details – how someone tips a waiter, what delights a person, the hidden messages in clothes. Find people's idols, the things they worship and will do anything to get – perhaps you can be the supplier of their fantasies. Remember: Since we all try to hide our weaknesses, there is little to be learned from our conscious behavior. What oozes out in the little things outside our conscious control is what you want to know.

Find the Helpless Child. Most weaknesses begin in childhood, before the self builds up compensatory defenses. Perhaps the child was pampered or indulged in a particular area, or perhaps a certain emotional need went unfulfilled; as he or she grows older, the indulgence or the deficiency may be buried but never disappears. Knowing about a childhood need gives you a powerful key to a person's weakness.

One sign of this weakness is that when you touch on it the person will often act like a child. Be on the lookout, then, for any behavior that should have been outgrown.

Look for Contrasts. An overt trait often conceals its opposite. People who thump their chests are often big cowards; the uptight are often screaming for adventure. By probing beyond appearances, you will often find people's weaknesses in the opposite of the qualities they reveal to you.

Fill the Void. The two main emotional voids to fill are insecurity and unhappiness. The insecure are suckers for any kind of social validation; as for the chronically unhappy, look for the roots of their unhappiness. The insecure and the unhappy are the people least able to disguise their weaknesses. The ability to fill their emotional voids is a great source of power, and an indefinitely prolongable one.

"What!" said he, "with your strength and agility, is it possible that you will yield to a feeble chamois? You have only to will, and you will be able to work wonders. Though the abyss be deep, yet, if you are only in earnest, I am certain you will clear it. Surely you can confide in my disinterested friendship. I would not expose your life to danger if I were not so well aware of your strength and dexterity." The lion's blood waxed hot, and began to boil in his veins. He flung himself with all his might into space. But he could not clear the chasm; so down he tumbled headlong, and was killed by the fall. Then what did his dear

Feed on Uncontrollable Emotions. The uncontrollable emotion can be a paranoid fear – a fear disproportionate to the situation – or any base motive such as lust, greed, vanity, or hatred. People in the grip of these emotions often cannot control themselves, and you can do the controlling for them.

Image: The Thumbscrew
Your enemy has secrets that he guards, thinks thoughts he will not reveal. But they come out in ways he cannot help. It is there somewhere, a groove of weakness on his head, at his heart, over his belly. Once you find the groove, put your thumb in it and turn him at will.

Authority: Find out each man's thumbscrew. 'Tis the art of setting their wills in action. It needs more skill than resolution. You must know where to get at anyone. Every volition has a special motive which varies according to taste. All men are idolaters, some of fame, others of self-interest, most of pleasure. Skill consists in knowing these idols in order to bring them into play. Knowing any man's mainspring of motive you have as it were the key to his will. (Baltasar Gracian, 1601–1658)

BE ROYAL IN YOUR OWN FASHION: ACT LIKE A KING TO BE TREATED LIKE ONE

JUDGMENT

The way you carry yourself will often determine how you are treated: in the long run, appearing vulgar or common will make people disrespect you. For a king respects himself, and inspires the same sentiment in others. By acting regally and confident of your powers, you make yourself seem destined to wear a crown.

As children, we start our lives with great exuberance, expecting and demanding everything from the world. This generally carries over into our first forays into society, as we begin our careers. But as we grow older the rebuffs and failures we experience set up boundaries that only get firmer with time. Coming to expect less from the world, we accept limitations that are really self-imposed. We start to bow and scrape and apologize for even the simplest of requests. The solution to such a shrinking of horizons is to deliberately force ourselves in the opposite direction – to downplay the failures and ignore the limitations, to make ourselves demand and expect as much as the child. To accomplish this, we must use a particular strategy upon ourselves. Call it the Strategy of the Crown.

The Strategy of the Crown is based on a simple chain of cause and effect: If we believe we are destined for great things, our belief will radiate outward, just as a crown creates an aura around a king. This outward radiance will infect the people around us, who will think we must have reasons to feel so confident.

Throughout history, people of undistinguished birth – the Theodoras of Byzantium, the Columbuses, the Beethovens, the Disraelis – have managed to work the Strategy of the Crown, believing so firmly in their own greatness that it becomes a self-fulfilling prophecy. The trick is simple: Be overcome by your self-belief. Even while you know you are practicing a kind of deception on yourself, act like a king. You are likely to be treated as one.

With all great deceivers there is a noteworthy occurrence to which they owe their power. In the actual act of deception they are overcome by belief in themselves: it is this which then speaks so miraculously and compellingly to those around them.

FRIEDRICH
NIETZSCHE,
1844–1900

The crown may separate you from other people, but it is up to you to make that separation real: you have to act differently, demonstrating your distance from those around you. One way to emphasize your difference is to always act with dignity, no matter the circumstance.

Regal bearing should not be confused with arrogance. Arrogance may seem the king's entitlement, but in fact it betrays insecurity. It is the very opposite of a royal demeanor.

Dignity, in fact, is invariably the mask to assume under difficult circumstances: it is as if nothing can affect you, and you have all the time in the world to respond. This is an extremely powerful pose.

Finally, to reinforce the inner psychological tricks involved in projecting a royal demeanor, there are outward strategies to help you create the effect. First, the Columbus Strategy: Always make a bold demand. Set your price high and do not waver. Second, in a dignified way, go after the highest person in the building. This immediately puts you on the same plane as the chief executive you are attacking. It is the David and Goliath Strategy: By choosing a great opponent, you create the appearance of greatness.

Third, give a gift of some sort to those above you. This is the strategy of those who have a patron: By giving your patron a gift, you are essentially saying that the two of you are equal.

Remember: it is up to you to set your own price. Ask for less and that is just what you will get. Ask for more, however, and you send a signal that you are worth a king's

Never lose your self-respect, nor be too familiar with yourself when you are alone. Let your integrity itself be your own standard of rectitude, and be more indebted to the severity of your own judgment of yourself than to all external precepts. Desist from unseemly conduct, rather out of respect for your own virtue than for the strictures of external authority. Come to hold yourself in awe, and you will have no need of Seneca's imaginary tutor.

BALTASAR
GRACIÁN,
1601–1658

ransom. Even those who turn you down respect you for your confidence, and that respect will eventually pay off in ways you cannot imagine.

Image: The Crown. Place it upon your head and you assume a different pose – tranquil yet radiating assurance. Never show doubt, never lose your dignity beneath the crown, or it will not fit. It will seem to be destined for one more worthy. Do not wait for a coronation; the greatest emperors crown themselves.

Authority: Everyone should be royal after his own fashion. Let all your actions, even though they are not those of a king, be, in their own sphere, worthy of one. Be sublime in your deeds, lofty in your thoughts; and in all your doings show that you deserve to be a king even though you are not one in reality. (Baltasar Gracian, 1601–1658)

MASTER THE ART
OF TIMING

JUDGMENT

*Never seem to be in a hurry – hurrying betrays a lack of
control over yourself, and over time. Always seem patient,
as if you know that everything will come to you eventually. Become a detective of the right moment; sniff out the
spirit of the times, the trends that will carry you to power.
Learn to stand back when the time is not yet ripe, and to
strike fiercely when it has reached fruition.*

Time is an artificial concept that we ourselves have created to make the limitlessness of eternity and the universe more bearable, more human. Since we have constructed the concept of time, we are also able to mold it to some degree, to play tricks with it. The time of a child is long and slow, with vast expanses; the time of an adult whizzes by frighteningly fast. Time, then, depends on perception, which, we know, can be willfully altered. This is the first thing to understand in mastering the art of timing.

There are three kinds of time for us to deal with; each presents problems that can be solved with skill and practice. First there is *long time*: the drawn-out, years-long kind of time that must be managed with patience and gentle guidance. Next there is *forced time*: the short-term time that we can manipulate as an offensive weapon, upsetting the timing of our opponents. Finally there is *end time*, when a plan must be executed with speed and force. We have waited, found the moment, and must not hesitate.

Long time. When you force the pace out of fear and impatience, you create a nest of problems that require fixing, and you end up taking much longer than if you had taken your time. Hurriers may occasionally get there quicker, but new dangers arise, and they find themselves in constant crisis mode, fixing the problems that they themselves have created. Sometimes not acting in the face of danger is your best move – you wait, you deliberately slow down. As time passes it will eventually present opportunities you

The sultan [of Persia] had sentenced two men to death. One of them, knowing how much the sultan loved his stallion, offered to teach the horse to fly within a year in return for his life. The sultan, fancying himself as the rider of the only flying horse in the world, agreed. The other prisoner looked at his friend in disbelief. "You know horses don't fly. What made you come up with a crazy idea like that? You're only postponing the inevitable." "Not so," said the [first prisoner]. "I have actually given myself four chances for freedom. First, the sultan might die during the year. Second, I might die. Third, the horse might die. And fourth

had not imagined.

You do not deliberately slow time down to live longer, or to take more pleasure in the moment, but the better to play the game of power. When your mind is uncluttered by constant emergencies you will see farther into the future. You will also be able to resist the baits that people dangle in front of you, and will keep yourself from becoming another impatient sucker. To build your power's foundation can take years; make sure that foundation is secure. Do not be a flash in the pan – success that is built up slowly and surely is the only kind that lasts.

Forcing time. The trick in forcing time is to upset the timing of others – to make them hurry, to make them wait, to make them abandon their own pace, to distort their perception of time. By upsetting the timing of your opponent while you stay patient, you open up time for yourself, which is half the game.

Making people wait is a powerful way of forcing time, as long as they do not figure out what you are up to. You control the clock, they linger in limbo – and rapidly come unglued, opening up opportunities for you to strike. The opposite effect is equally powerful: you make your opponents hurry. Start off your dealings with them slowly, then suddenly apply pressure, making them feel that everything is happening at once. People who lack the time to think will make mistakes – so set their deadlines for them.

End time. You can play the game with the utmost artistry – waiting patiently for the

... I might teach the horse to fly!"

STORY RELATED IN R. G. H. SIU, THE CRAFT OF POWER, 1979

right moment to act, putting your competitors off their form by messing with their timing – but it won't mean a thing unless you know how to finish. Patience is worthless unless combined with a willingness to fall ruthlessly on your opponent at the right moment. You can wait as long as necessary for the conclusion to come, but when it comes it must come quickly. Use speed to paralyze your opponent.

Image: The Hawk. Patiently and silently it circles the sky, high above, all-seeing with its powerful eyes. Those below have no awareness that they are being tracked. Suddenly, when the moment arrives, the hawk swoops down with a speed that cannot be defended against; before its prey knows what has happened, the bird's vicelike talons have carried it up into the sky.

Authority: There is a tide in the affairs of men, / Which, taken at the flood, leads on to fortune; / Omitted, all the voyage of their life / Is bound in shallows and in miseries. (*Julius Caesar*, William Shakespeare, 1564–1616)

DISDAIN THINGS
YOU CANNOT HAVE:
IGNORING THEM IS
THE BEST REVENGE

JUDGMENT

By acknowledging a petty problem you give it existence and credibility. The more attention you pay an enemy, the stronger you make him; and a small mistake is often made worse and more visible when you try to fix it. It is sometimes best to leave things alone. If there is something you want but cannot have, show contempt for it. The less interest you reveal, the more superior you seem.

Desire often creates paradoxical effects: the more you want something, the more you chase after it, the more it eludes you. The more interest you show, the more you repel the object of your desire. This is because your interest is too strong – it makes people awkward, even fearful. Uncontrollable desire makes you seem weak, unworthy, pathetic.

You need to turn your back on what you want, show your contempt and disdain. This is the kind of powerful response that will drive your targets crazy. They will respond with a desire of their own, which is simply to have an effect on you – perhaps to possess you, perhaps to hurt you. If they want to possess you, you have successfully completed the first step of seduction. If they want to hurt you, you have unsettled them and made them play by your rules.

Contempt is the prerogative of the king. Where his eyes turn, what he decides to see, is what has reality; what he ignores and turns his back on is as good as dead. That was the weapon of King Louis XIV – if he did not like you, he acted as if you were not there, maintaining his superiority by cutting off the dynamic of interaction. This is the power you have when you play the card of contempt, periodically showing people that you can do without them.

If choosing to ignore enhances your power, it follows that the opposite approach – commitment and engagement – often weakens you. By paying undue attention to a puny enemy, *you* look puny, and the longer it takes you to crush such an enemy, the larger the enemy seems.

Once when G. K. Chesteron's economic views were abused in print by George Bernard Shaw, his friends waited in vain for him to reply. Historian Hilaire Belloc reproached him. "My dear Belloc," Chesterton said, "I have answered him. To a man of Shaw's wit, silence is the one unbearable repartee."

QUOTED IN CLIFTON FADIMAN, ED., THE LITTLE, BROWN BOOK OF ANECDOTES, 1985

A second danger: If you succeed in crushing the irritant, or even if you merely wound it, you create sympathy for the weaker side.

It is tempting to want to fix our mistakes, but the harder we try, the worse we often make them. It is sometimes more politic to leave them alone. Instead of inadvertently focusing attention on a problem, making it seem worse by publicizing how much concern and anxiety it is causing you, it is often far wiser to play the contemptuous aristocrat, not deigning to acknowledge the problem's existence. There are several ways to execute this strategy.

First there is the sour-grapes approach. If there is something you want but that you realize you cannot have, the worst thing you can do is draw attention to your disappointment by complaining about it. An infinitely more powerful tactic is to act as if it never really interested you in the first place.

Second, when you are attacked by an inferior, deflect people's attention by making it clear that the attack has not even registered. Look away, or answer sweetly, showing how little the attack concerns you. Similarly, when you yourself have committed a blunder, the best response is often to make less of your mistake by treating it lightly.

Remember: The powerful responses to niggling, petty annoyances and irritations are contempt and disdain. Never show that something has affected you, or that you are offended – that only shows you have acknowledged a problem. Contempt is a dish that is best served cold and without affectation.

Nay, with most people there will be no harm in occasionally mixing a grain of disdain with your treatment of them; that will make them value your friendship all the more. Chi non istima vien stimato, *as a subtle Italian proverb has it – to disregard is to win regard. But if we really think very highly of a person, we should conceal it from him like a crime. This is not a very gratifying thing to do, but it is right. Why, a dog will not bear being treated too kindly, let alone a man!*

ARTHUR SCHOPENHAUER, 1788–1860

Image:
The Tiny Wound.

It is small but painful
and irritating. You try
all sorts of medicaments,
you complain, you scratch
and pick at the scab. Doctors
only make it worse, transform-
ing the tiny wound into a grave
matter. If only you had left the
wound alone, letting time heal it
and freeing yourself of worry.

Authority: Know how to play the
card of contempt. It is the most
politic kind of revenge. For there
are many of whom we should
have known nothing if their distinguished opponents had taken
no notice of them. There is no
revenge like oblivion, for it is the
entombment of the unworthy in
the dust of their own nothingness.
(Baltasar Gracián, 1601–1658)

CREATE COMPELLING

SPECTACLES

JUDGMENT

Striking imagery and grand symbolic gestures create the aura of power – everyone responds to them. Stage spectacles for those around you, then, full of arresting visuals and radiant symbols that heighten your presence. Dazzled by appearances, no one will notice what you are really doing.

Using words to plead your case is a risky business: words are dangerous instruments, and often go astray. The words people use to persuade us virtually invite us to reflect on them with words of our own; we mull them over, and often end up believing the opposite of what they say. (That is part of our perverse nature.) It also happens that words offend us, stirring up associations unintended by the speaker.

The visual, on the other hand, short-circuits the labyrinth of words. It strikes with an emotional power and immediacy that leave no gaps for reflection and doubt. Like music, it leaps right over rational, reasonable thoughts.

Understand: Words put you on the defensive. If you have to explain yourself your power is already in question. The image, on the other hand, imposes itself as a given. It discourages questions, creates forceful associations, resists unintended interpretations, communicates instantly, and forges bonds that transcend social differences. Words stir up arguments and divisions; images bring people together. They are the quintessential instruments of power.

The symbol has the same force, whether it is visual or a verbal description of something visual (the words "the Sun King"). The symbolic object stands for something else, something abstract. The abstract concept – purity, patriotism, courage, love – is full of emotional and powerful associations.

The Roman Emperor Constantine worshipped the sun as a god for most of his life; one day, though, he looked up at the sun,

Because of the light it shines on the other stars which make up a kind of court around it, because of the just and equal distribution of its rays to all alike, because of the good it brings to all places, producing life, joy and action, because of its constancy from which it never varies, I chose the sun as the most magnificent image to represent a great leader.

LOUIS XIV, THE
SUN KING,
1638–1715

and saw a cross superimposed on it. The vision of the cross over the sun proved to him the ascendancy of the new religion, and he converted not just himself but the whole Roman Empire to Christianity soon thereafter. All the preaching and proselytizing in the world could not have been as powerful. Find and associate yourself with the images and symbols that will communicate in this immediate way today, and you will have untold power.

Most effective of all is a new combination – a fusion of images and symbols that have not been seen together before, but that through their association clearly demonstrate your new idea, message, religion. The creation of new images and symbols out of old ones in this way has a poetic effect – viewers' associations run rampant, giving them a sense of participation.

Use the power of symbols as a way to rally, animate, and unite your troops or team. During the rebellion against the French crown in 1648, those loyal to the king disparaged the rebels by comparing them to the slingshots (in French, *frondes*) that little boys use to frighten big boys. Cardinal Retz decided to turn this disparaging term into the rebels' symbol: the uprising was now known as the *Fronde*, and the rebels as *frondeurs*. They began to wear sashes in their hats that symbolized the slingshot, and the word became their rallying cry. Without it the rebellion might well have petered out. Always find a symbol to represent your cause – the more emotional associations, the better.

The best way to use images and symbols

There was a man named Sakamotoya Hechigwan who lived in upper Kyoto ... When [Emperor] Hideyoshi gave his great [tea ceremony] meeting in the tenth month of 1588, Hechigwan set up a great red umbrella nine feet across mounted on a stick seven feet high. The circumference of the handle he surrounded for about two feet by a reed fence in such a way that the rays of the sun were reflected from it and diffused the colour of the umbrella all around. This device pleased Hideyoshi so much that he remitted Hechigwan's taxes as a reward.

A.L. SADLER, CHA-NO-YU: THE JAPANESE TEA CEREMONY, 1933

is to organize them into a grand spectacle that awes people and distracts them from unpleasant realities. This is easy to do: people love what is grand, spectacular, and larger than life. Appeal to their emotions and they will flock to your spectacle in hordes. The visual is the easiest route to their hearts.

Image:
The Cross and
the Sun. Crucifixion
and total radiance. With
one imposed over the
other, a new reality takes
shape – a new power is in
the ascendant. The
symbol – no explana-
tion necessary.

Authority: The people are always impressed by the superficial appearance of things ... The [prince] should, at fitting times of the year, keep the people occupied and distracted with festivities and spectacles. (Niccolò Machiavelli, 1469–1527)

THINK AS YOU LIKE
BUT BEHAVE LIKE
OTHERS

JUDGMENT

If you make a show of going against the times, flaunting your unconventional ideas and unorthodox ways, people will think that you only want attention and that you look down upon them. They will find a way to punish you for making them feel inferior. It is far safer to blend in and nurture the common touch. Share your originality only with tolerant friends and those who are sure to appreciate your uniqueness.

*"Look around
you,"* said the
citizen. *"This is
the largest
market in the
world."*
"Oh surely not,"
said the traveller.
*"Well, perhaps
not the largest,"*
said the citizen,
*"but much the
best."*
*"You are
certainly wrong
there,"* said the
traveller. *"I can
tell you ..."*
They buried the
stranger in the
dusk.

FABLES, ROBERT
LOUIS
STEVENSON,
1850–1894

KEYS TO POWER

We all tell lies and hide our true feelings, for complete free expression is a social impossibility. From an early age we learn to conceal our thoughts, telling the prickly and insecure what we know they want to hear, watching carefully lest we offend them. For most of us this is natural – there are ideas and values that most people accept, and it is pointless to argue. We believe what we want to, then, but on the outside we wear a mask.

There are people, however, who see such restraints as an intolerable infringement on their freedom, and who have a need to prove the superiority of their values and beliefs. In the end, though, their arguments convince only a few and offend a great deal more. The reason arguments do not work is that most people hold their ideas and values without thinking about them. There is a strong emotional content in their beliefs: they really do not want to have to rework their habits of thinking, and when you challenge them, whether directly through your arguments or indirectly through your behavior, they are hostile.

Wise and clever people learn early on that they can display conventional behavior and mouth conventional ideas without having to believe in them. The power these people gain from blending in is that of being left alone to have the thoughts they want to have, and to express them to the people they want to express them to, without suffering isolation or ostracism. Once they have established themselves in a position of power, they can try to convince a wider circle of the correctness of their ideas – perhaps working indirectly.

Do not be so foolish as to imagine that in our own time the old orthodoxies are gone. Jonas Salk, for instance, thought science had gotten past politics and protocol. And so, in his search for a polio vaccine, he broke all the rules – going public with a discovery before showing it to the scientific community, taking credit for the vaccine without acknowledging the scientists who had paved the way, making himself a star. The public may have loved him but scientists shunned him. His disrespect for his community's orthodoxies left him isolated, and he wasted years trying to heal the breach, and struggling for funding and cooperation.

Not only do people of power avoid the offense of Salk, they also learn to play the clever fox and feign the common touch. This has been the ploy of con artists and politicians throughout the centuries. Leaders like Julius Caesar and Franklin D. Roosevelt have overcome their natural aristocratic stance to cultivate a familiarity with the common man. They have expressed this familiarity in little gestures, often symbolic, to show the people that their leaders share popular values, despite their different status.

The logical extension of this practice is the invaluable ability to be all things to all people. When you go into society, leave behind your own ideas and values, and put on the mask that is most appropriate for the group in which you find yourself. Bismarck played this game successfully for years – there were people who vaguely understood what he was up to, but not clearly enough that it mattered. People will swallow the bait because it flatters them to believe that you

If Machiavelli had had a prince for disciple, the first thing he would have recommended him to do would have been to write a book against Machiavellism.

VOLTAIRE,
1694–1778

share their ideas. They will not take you as a hypocrite if you are careful – for how can they accuse you of hypocrisy if you do not let them know exactly what you stand for? Nor will they see you as lacking in values. Of course you have values – the values you share with them, while in their company.

Image:
The Black Sheep. The herd shuns the black sheep, uncertain whether or not it belongs with them. So it straggles behind, or wanders away from the herd, where it is cornered by wolves and promptly devoured. Stay with the herd – there is safety in numbers. Keep your differences in your thoughts and not in your fleece.

Authority: Do not give dogs what is holy; and do not throw your pearls before swine, lest they trample them under foot and turn to attack you. (Jesus Christ, Matthew 7:6)

STIR UP WATERS
TO CATCH FISH

JUDGMENT

Anger and emotion are strategically counterproductive. You must always stay calm and objective. But if you can make your enemies angry while staying calm yourself, you gain a decided advantage. Put your enemies off-balance: find the chink in their vanity through which you can rattle them and you hold the strings.

If possible, no
animosity should
be felt for
anyone ... To
speak angrily to
a person, to
show your
hatred by what
you say or by the
way you look, is
an unnecessary
proceeding –
dangerous,
foolish,
ridiculous, and
vulgar.
Anger or hatred
should never be
shown otherwise
than in what you
do; and feelings
will be all the
more effective in
action, in so far
as you avoid the
exhibition of
them in any
other way. It is
only the cold-
blooded animals
whose bite is
poisonous.

ARTHUR
SCHOPENHAUER,
1788–1860

Angry people usually end up looking ridiculous, for their response seems out of proportion to what occasioned it. They have taken
things too seriously, exaggerating the hurt or
insult that has been done to them. They are
so sensitive to slight that it becomes comical
how much they take personally. More comical still is their belief that their outbursts sig-
nify power. The truth is the opposite:
Petulance is not power, it is a sign of help-
lessness. People may temporarily be cowed
by your tantrums, but in the end they lose
respect for you. They also realize they can
easily undermine a person with so little self-
control.

The answer, however, is not to repress
our angry or emotional responses. For
repression drains us of energy and pushes us
into strange behavior. Instead we have to
change our perspective: we have to realize
that nothing in the social realm, and in the
game of power, is personal.

Everyone is caught up in a chain of
events that long predates the present
moment. Our anger often stems from problems in our childhood, from the problems of
our parents which stem from their own childhood, on and on. Our anger also has roots in
the many interactions with others, the accu-
mulated disappointments and heartaches
that we have suffered. An individual will
often appear as the instigator of our anger
but it is much more complicated, goes far
beyond what that individual did to us. If a
person explodes with anger at you (and it
seems out of proportion to what you did to
them), you must remind yourself that it is not

exclusively directed at you – do not be so vain. The cause is much larger, goes way back in time, involves dozens of prior hurts, and is actually not worth the bother to understand. Instead of seeing it as a personal grudge, look at the emotional outburst as a disguised power move, an attempt to control or punish you cloaked in the form of hurt feelings and anger.

This shift of perspective will let you play the game of power with more clarity and energy. Instead of overreacting, and becoming ensnared in people's emotions, you will turn their loss of control to your advantage.

During an important battle in the War of the Three Kingdoms, in the third century A.D., advisers to the commander Ts'ao Ts'ao discovered documents showing that certain of his generals had conspired with the enemy, and urged him to arrest and execute them. Instead he ordered the documents burned and the matter forgotten. At this critical moment in the battle, to get upset or demand justice would have reverberated against him: an angry action would have called attention to the generals' disloyalty, which would have harmed the troops' morale. Justice could wait – he would deal with the generals in time. Ts'ao Ts'ao kept his head and made the right decision.

Anger only cuts off our options, and the powerful cannot thrive without options. Once you train yourself not to take matters personally, and to control your emotional responses, you will have placed yourself in a position of tremendous power: now you can play with the emotional responses of other people. Stir the insecure into action by

Kin'yo, an officer of the second rank, had a brother called the High Priest Ryogaku, an extremely bad-tempered man. Next to his monastery grew a large nettle-tree which occasioned the nickname people gave him, the Nettle-tree High Priest. "That name is outrageous," said the high priest, and cut down the tree. The stump still being left, people referred to him now as the Stump High Priest. More furious than ever, Ryogaku had the stump dug up and thrown away, but this left a big ditch. People now called him the Ditch High Priest.

ESSAYS IN IDLENESS, KENKO, JAPAN, FOURTEENTH CENTURY

impugning their manhood, and by dangling the prospect of an easy victory before their faces.

In the face of a hot-headed enemy, finally, an excellent response is no response. Nothing is as infuriating as a man who keeps his cool while others are losing theirs. If it will work to your advantage to unsettle people, affect the aristocratic, bored pose, neither mocking nor triumphant but simply indifferent. This will light their fuse. When they embarrass themselves with a temper tantrum, you will have gained several victories, one of these being that in the face of their childishness you have maintained your dignity and composure.

Image: The Pond of Fish.
The waters are clear and calm, and
the fish are well below the surface.
Stir the waters and they emerge.
Stir it some more and they get
angry, rising to the surface, biting
whatever comes near – including a
freshly baited hook.

Authority: If your opponent is of a hot temper, try to irritate him. If he is arrogant, try to encourage his egotism … One who is skilled at making the enemy move does so by creating a situation according to which the enemy will act; he entices the enemy with something he is certain to take. He keeps the enemy on the move by holding out bait and then attacks him with picked troops. (Sun-tzu, fourth century B.C.)

LAW
40

DESPISE THE
FREE LUNCH

JUDGMENT

What is offered for free is dangerous – it usually involves either a trick or a hidden obligation. What has worth is worth paying for. By paying your own way you stay clear of gratitude, guilt, and deceit. It is also often wise to pay the full price – there is no cutting corners with excellence. Be lavish with your money and keep it circulating, for generosity is a sign and a magnet for power.

A miser, to make sure of his property, sold all that he had and converted it into a great lump of gold, which he hid in a hole in the ground, and went continually to visit and inspect it. This roused the curiosity of one of his workmen, who, suspecting that there was a treasure, when his master's back was turned, went to the spot, and stole it away. When the miser returned and found the place empty, he wept and tore his hair. But a neighbor who saw him in this extravagant grief, and learned the cause of it, said: "Fret thyself no longer, but take a stone and put it in the same place, and think that it is your lump of gold; for, as you never meant to use it, the one

MONEY AND POWER

In the realm of power, everything must be judged by its cost, and everything has a price. What is offered for free or at bargain rates often comes with a psychological price tag – complicated feelings of obligation, compromises with quality, the insecurity those compromises bring, on and on. The powerful learn early to protect their most valuable resources: independence and room to maneuver. By paying the full price, they keep themselves free of dangerous entanglements and worries.

Being open and flexible with money also teaches the value of strategic generosity, a variation on the old trick of "giving when you are about to take." By giving the appropriate gift, you put the recipient under obligation. Generosity softens people up – to be deceived. By gaining a reputation for liberality, you win people's admiration while distracting them from your power plays.

For everyone able to play with money, thousands more are locked in a self-destructive refusal to use money creatively and strategically. These types represent the opposite pole to the powerful, and you must learn to recognize them – either to avoid their poisonous natures or to turn their inflexibility to your advantage:

The Greedy Fish. The greedy fish take the human side out of money. Cold and ruthless, they see only the lifeless balance sheet; viewing others solely as either pawns or obstructions in their pursuit of wealth, they trample on people's sentiments and alienate valuable allies. No one wants to work with the greedy fish, and over the years they end up isolated, which often proves their undoing. They are also easy to deceive: simply lure them with the bait of easy money, and they will swallow the ruse hook, line, and sinker. Either avoid them before they exploit you or play on their greed to your gain.

The Bargain Demon. Powerful people judge everything by what it costs, not just in money but in time, dignity, and peace of mind. And this is exactly what Bargain Demons cannot do. Wasting valuable time digging for bargains, they worry endlessly about what they could have gotten elsewhere for a little less. On top of that, the bargain item they do buy is often shabby; perhaps it needs costly repairs, or will have to be replaced twice as fast as a high-quality item. These types might seem to harm only themselves, but their attitudes are contagious.

The Sadist. Financial sadists play vicious power games with money as a way of asserting their power. They might, for example, make you wait for money that is owed you, promising you that the check is in the mail. Sadists seem to think that paying for something gives them the right to torture and abuse the seller. They have no sense of the courtier element in money. If you are unlucky enough to get involved with this type, accepting a financial loss may be better in the long run than getting entangled in their destructive power games.

The Indiscriminate Giver. Generosity has a definite function in power: it attracts

will do you as much good as the other."
The worth of money is not in its possession, but in its use.

FABLES, AESOP,
SIXTH CENTURY
B.C.

people, softens them up, makes allies out of
them. But it has to be used strategically, with
a definite end in mind. Indiscriminate
Givers, on the other hand, are generous
because they want to be loved and admired
by all. And their generosity is so indiscriminate and needy that it may not have the
desired effect: if they give to one and all, why
should the recipient feel special? Attractive
as it may seem to make an Indiscriminate
Giver your mark, in any involvement with
this type you will often feel burdened by
their insatiable emotional needs.

Image: The River. To protect
yourself or to save the resource,
you dam it up. Soon, however,
the waters become dank and
pestilent. Only the foulest forms
of life can live in such stagnant
waters; nothing travels on them,
all commerce stops. Destroy the
dam. When water flows and
circulates, it generates abun-
dance, wealth, and power in
ever larger circles. The River
must flood periodically for
good things to flourish.

Authority: The great man who is a miser is a great fool, and a man in high places can have no vice so harmful as avarice. A miserly man can conquer neither lands nor lordships, for he does not have a plentiful supply of friends with whom he may work his will. Whoever wants to have friends must not love his possessions but must acquire friends by means of fair gifts; for in the same way that the lodestone subtly draws iron to itself, so the gold and silver that a man gives attract the hearts of men. (*The Romance of the Rose*, Guillaume de Lorris, c. 1200–1238)

AVOID STEPPING INTO
A GREAT MAN'S SHOES

JUDGMENT

What happens first always appears better and more original than what comes after. If you succeed a great man or have a famous parent, you will have to accomplish double their achievements to outshine them. Do not get lost in their shadow, or stuck in a past not of your own making: establish your own name and identity by changing course. Slay the overbearing father, disparage his legacy, and gain power by shining in your own way.

KEYS TO POWER

In many ancient kingdoms, for example Bengal and Sumatra, after the king had ruled for several years his subjects would execute him. This was done partly as a ritual of renewal, but also to prevent him from growing too powerful. Now that he was no longer around for his honors to go to his head, he could be worshipped as a god. Meanwhile the field had been cleared for a new and youthful order to establish itself.

The ambivalent, hostile attitude towards the king or father figure also finds expression in legends of heroes who do not know their father. Moses, the archetypal man of power, was found abandoned among the bulrushes and never knew his parents; without a father to compete with him or limit him, he could attain the heights of power. Later in his life Alexander the Great spread the story that the god Jupiter Ammon had sired him, not Philip of Macedon. Legends and rituals like these eliminate the human father because he symbolizes the destructive power of the past.

The past prevents the young hero from creating his own world – he must do as his father did, even after that father is dead or powerless. The hero must bow and scrape before his predecessor and yield to tradition and precedent.

Power depends on the ability to fill a void, to occupy a field that has been cleared of the dead weight of the past. Only after the father-figure has been properly done away with will you have the necessary space to create and establish a new order. There are several strategies you can adopt to accomplish this.

Many would have shone like the very phoenix in their occupations if others had not preceded them. Being first is a great advantage; with eminence, twice as good. Deal the first hand and you will win the upper ground ... Those who go first win fame by right of birth, and those who follow are like second sons, contenting themselves with meager portions ... Solomon opted wisely for pacifism, yielding warlike things to his father. By changing course he found it easier to become a hero ... And our great Philip II governed the entire world from the throne of his prudence,

astonishing the
ages. If his
unconquered
father was a
model of energy,
Philip was a
paradigm of
prudence ... This
sort of novelty
has helped the
well-advised win
a place in the roll
of the great.
Without leaving
their own art, the
ingenious leave
the common path
and take, even in
professions gray
with age, new
steps toward
eminence.
Horace yielded
epic poetry to
Virgil, and
Martial the lyric
to Horace.
Terence opted for
comedy, Persius
for satire, each
hoping to be first
in his genre. Bold
fancy never
succumbed to
facile imitation.

BALTASAR
GRACIAN, A
POCKET MIRROR
FOR HEROES,
TRANSLATED BY
CHRISTOPHER
MAURER, 1996

Perhaps the simplest way to escape the shadow of the past is simply to belittle it, playing on the timeless antagonism between the generations, stirring up the young against the old. For this you need a convenient older figure to pillory.

The distance you establish from your predecessor often demands some symbolism, a way of advertising itself publicly. Louis XIV, for example, created such symbolism when he rejected the traditional palace of the French kings and built his own palace of Versailles. Follow his example: never let yourself be seen as following your predecessor's path. If you do you will never surpass him. You must physically demonstrate your difference, by establishing a style and symbolism that sets you apart.

There is a kind of stubborn stupidity that recurs throughout history, and is a strong impediment to power: the superstitious belief that if the person before you succeeded by doing A, B, and C, you can re-create their success by doing the same thing. This cookie-cutter approach will seduce the uncreative, for it is easy, and appeals to their timidity and their laziness. But circumstances never repeat themselves exactly. You must adopt a ruthless strategy toward the past: burn all the books of your predecessors, and train yourself to react to circumstances as they happen.

Finally, plenitude and prosperity tend to make us lazy and inactive: when our power is secure we have no need to act. This is a serious danger. You must be prepared to return to square one psychologically rather than growing fat and lazy with prosperity.

How often our early triumphs turn us into a kind of caricature of ourselves. Powerful people recognize these traps; they struggle constantly to re-create themselves. The father must not be allowed to return; he must be slain at every step of the way.

Image: The Father. He casts a giant shadow over his children, keeping them in thrall long after he is gone by tying them to the past, squashing their youthful spirit, and forcing them down the same tired path he followed himself. His tricks are many. At every crossroads you must slay the father and step out of his shadow.

Authority: Beware of stepping into a great man's shoes – you will have to accomplish twice as much to surpass him. Those who follow are taken for imitators. No matter how much they sweat, they will never shed that burden. It is an uncommon skill to find a new path for excellence, a modern route to celebrity. There are many roads to singularity, not all of them well traveled. The newest ones can be arduous, but they are often shortcuts to greatness. (Baltasar Gracián, 1601–1658)

STRIKE THE SHEPHERD
AND THE SHEEP
WILL SCATTER

JUDGMENT

Trouble can often be traced to a single strong individual – the stirrer, the arrogant underling, the poisoner of good will. If you allow such people room to operate, others will succumb to their influence. Do not wait for the troubles they cause to multiply, do not try to negotiate with them – they are irredeemable. Neutralize their influence by isolating or banishing them. Strike at the source of the trouble and the sheep will scatter.

KEYS TO POWER

In the past, an entire nation would be ruled by a king and his handful of ministers. Only the elite had any power to play with. Over the centuries, power has gradually become more and more diffused and democratized. This has created, however, a common mis-perception that groups no longer have cen-ters of power – that power is spread out and scattered among many people. Actually, however, power has changed in its numbers but not in its essence. There may be fewer mighty tyrants commanding the power of life and death over millions, but there remain thousands of petty tyrants ruling smaller realms, and enforcing their will through indi-rect power games, charisma, and so on. In every group, power is concentrated in the hands of one or two people, for this is one area in which human nature will never change: people will congregate around a sin-gle strong personality like stars orbiting a sun.

To labor under the illusion that this kind of power center no longer exists is to make endless mistakes, waste energy and time. Powerful people never waste time. Out-wardly they may play along with the game – pretending that power is shared among many – but inwardly they keep their eyes on the inevitable few in the group who hold the cards. These are the ones they work on. When troubles arise, they look for the under-lying cause, the single strong character who started the stirring and whose isolation or banishment will settle the waters again.

In his family therapy practice, Dr Mil-ton Erickson found that if the family

When the tree falls, the monkeys scatter.

CHINESE SAYING

dynamic was unsettled and dysfunctional
there was inevitably one person who was the
stirrer, the troublemaker. In his sessions he
would symbolically isolate this rotten apple
by seating him or her apart from the others,
if only by a few feet. Slowly the other family
members would see the physically separate
person as the source of their difficulty. Once
you recognize who the stirrer is, pointing it
out to other people will accomplish a great
deal. Remember: Stirrers thrive by hiding in
the group, disguising their actions among the
reactions of others. Render their actions visible and they lose their power to upset.

A key element in games of strategy is
isolating the enemy's power. In chess you try
to corner the king. In the Chinese game of go
you try to isolate the enemy's forces in small
pockets, rendering them immobile and inef-
fectual. It is often better to isolate your enemies than to destroy them – you seem less
brutal. The result, though, is the same, for in
the game of power, isolation spells death.

The most effective form of isolation is
somehow to separate troublemakers from
their power base. When Mao Tse-tung
wanted to eliminate an enemy in the ruling
elite, he did not confront the person directly;
he silently and stealthily worked to isolate
the man, divide his allies and turn them away
from him, shrink his support. Soon the man
would vanish on his own.

Finally, the reason you strike at the
shepherd is because such an action will dis-
hearten the sheep beyond any rational measure. With the leader gone the center of
gravity is gone; there is nothing to revolve
around and everything falls apart. Aim at the

leaders, bring them down, and look for the endless opportunities in the confusion that will ensue.

Image: A Flock of Fatted Sheep. Do not waste precious time trying to steal a sheep or two; do not risk life and limb by setting upon the dogs that guard the flock. Aim at the shepherd. Lure him away and the dogs will follow. Strike him down and the flock will scatter – you can pick them off one by one.

Authority: If you draw a bow, draw the strongest. If you use an arrow, use the longest. To shoot a rider, first shoot his horse. To catch a gang of bandits, first capture its leader. Just as a country has its border, so the killing of men has its limits. If the enemy's attack can be stopped [with a blow to the head], why have any more dead and wounded than necessary? (Chinese poet Du Fu, Tang dynasty, eighth century)

WORK ON THE HEARTS
AND MINDS OF OTHERS

JUDGMENT

Coercion creates a reaction that will eventually work against you. You must seduce others into wanting to move in your direction. A person you have seduced becomes your loyal pawn. And the way to seduce others is to operate on their individual psychologies and weaknesses. Soften up the resistant by working on their emotions, playing on what they hold dear and what they fear. Ignore the hearts and minds of others and they will grow to hate you.

KEYS TO POWER

In the game of power, you are surrounded by people who have absolutely no reason to help you unless it is in their interest to do so. And if you have nothing to offer their self-interest, you are likely to make them hostile, for they will see in you just one more competitor, one more waster of their time. Those that overcome this prevailing coldness are the ones who find the key that unlocks the stranger's heart and mind, seducing him into their corner, if necessary softening him up for a punch. But most people never learn this side of the game. When they meet someone new, rather than stepping back and probing to see what makes this person unique, they talk about themselves, eager to impose their own willpower and prejudices. They may not know it but they are secretly creating an enemy, a resister, because there is no more infuriating feeling than having your individuality ignored, your own psychology unacknowledged.

Remember: The key to persuasion is softening people up and breaking them down, gently. Seduce them with a two-pronged approach: work on their emotions and play on their intellectual weaknesses. Be alert to both what separates them from everyone else (their individual psychology) and what they share with everyone else (their basic emotional responses). Aim at the primary emotions – love, hate, jealousy. Once you move their emotions you have reduced their control, making them more vulnerable to persuasion.

When T. E. Lawrence was fighting the Turks in the deserts of the Middle East

Governments saw men only in mass; but our men, being irregulars, were not formations, but individuals ... Our kingdoms lay in each man's mind.

SEVEN PILLARS OF WISDOM, T. E. LAWRENCE, 1888–1935

during World War I, he had an epiphany: it seemed to him that conventional warfare had lost its value. The old-fashioned soldier was lost in the enormous armies of the time, in which he was ordered about like a lifeless pawn. Lawrence wanted to turn this around. For him, every soldier's mind was a kingdom he had to conquer. A committed, psychologically motivated soldier would fight harder and more creatively than a puppet.

Lawrence's perception is still more true in the world today, where so many of us feel alienated, anonymous, and suspicious of authority, all of which makes overt power plays and force even more counter-productive and dangerous. Instead of manipulating lifeless pawns, make those on your side convinced and excited by the cause you have enlisted them in. And to accomplish this you need to deal with their individual psychologies. Never clumsily assume that the tactic that worked on one person will necessarily work on another.

The quickest way to secure people's minds is by demonstrating, as simply as possible, how an action will benefit them. Self-interest is the strongest motive of all: a great cause may capture minds, but once the first flush of excitement is over, interest will flag – unless there is something to be gained. Self-interest is the solider foundation.

The people who are best at appealing to people's minds are often artists, intellectuals, and those of a more poetic nature. This is because ideas are most easily communicated through metaphors and imagery. It is always good policy, then, to have in your pocket at least one artist or intellectual who can appeal concretely to people's minds.

Finally, learn to play the numbers game. The wider your support base the stronger your power. You too must constantly win over more allies on all levels – a time will inevitably come when you will need them.

Image: The
Keyhole. People
build walls to keep
you out; never force
your way in – you will
find only more walls
within walls. There are
doors in these walls,
doors to the heart and
mind, and they have tiny
keyholes. Peer through
the keyhole, find the key
that opens the door,
and you have access
to their will with no
ugly signs of
forced entry.

Authority: The difficulties in the way of persuasion lie in my knowing the heart of the per- suaded in order thereby to fit my wording into it ... For this reason, whoever attempts persuasion before the throne must carefully observe the sovereign's feelings of love and hate, his secret wishes and fears, before he can conquer his heart. (Han Fei Tzu, Chinese philosopher, third century B.C.)

DISARM AND INFURIATE
WITH THE MIRROR EFFECT

JUDGMENT

The mirror reflects reality, but it is also the perfect tool for deception: when you mirror your enemies, doing exactly as they do, they cannot figure out your strategy. The Mirror Effect mocks and humiliates them, making them overreact. By holding up a mirror to their psyches, you seduce them with the illusion that you share their values; by holding up a mirror to their actions, you teach them a lesson. Few can resist the power of the Mirror Effect.

MIRROR EFFECTS

Mirrors have the power to disturb us. Gazing at our reflection in the mirror, we most often see what we want to see – the image of ourselves with which we are most comfortable. We tend not to look too closely, ignoring the wrinkles and blemishes. But if we do look hard at the reflected image, we sometimes feel that we are seeing ourselves as others see us, as a person among other people, an object rather than a subject.

In using Mirror Effects we symbolically re-create this disturbing power by mirroring the actions of other people, mimicking their movements to unsettle and infuriate them. Made to feel mocked, cloned, objectlike, an image without a soul, they get angry. Or do the same thing slightly differently and they might feel disarmed – you have perfectly reflected their wishes and desires. The Effect contains great power because it operates on the most primitive emotions.

There are four main Mirror Effects in the realm of power:

The Neutralizing Effect. If you do what your enemies do, following their actions as best you can, they cannot see what you are up to – they are blinded by your mirror. Their strategy for dealing with you depends on your reacting to them in a way characteristic of you; neutralize it by playing a game of mimicry with them. The tactic has a mocking, even infuriating effect. Most of us remember the childhood experience of someone teasing us by repeating our words exactly – after a while, usually not long, we wanted to punch them in the face. Working

When you have come to grips and are striving together with the enemy, and you realize that you cannot advance, you "soak in" and become one with the enemy. You can win by applying a suitable technique while you are mutually entangled ... You can win often decisively with the advantage of knowing how to "soak" into the enemy, whereas, were you to draw apart, you would lose the chance to win.

MIYAMOTO MUSASHI, A BOOK OF FIVE RINGS, JAPAN, SIXTEENTH CENTURY

more subtly as an adult, you can still unsettle your opponents this way; shielding your own strategy with the mirror, you lay invisible traps, or push your opponents into the trap they planned for you.

The Narcissus Effect. All of us are profoundly in love with ourselves. The Narcissus Effect plays on this universal narcissism: you look deep into the souls of other people; fathom their innermost desires, their values, their tastes, their spirit; and you reflect it back to them, making yourself into a kind of mirror image. Your ability to reflect their psyche gives you great power over them; they may even feel a tinge of love.

The Moral Effect. With the Moral Effect, you teach others a lesson by giving them a taste of their own medicine. You mirror what they have done to you, and do so in a way that makes them realize you are doing to them exactly what they did to you. You make them feel that their behavior has been unpleasant, as opposed to hearing you complain and whine about it, which only gets their defenses up. And as they feel the result of their actions mirrored back at them, they realize in the profoundest sense how they hurt or punish others with their unsocial behavior.

The Hallucinatory Effect. Mirrors are tremendously deceptive, for they create a sense that you are looking at the real world. Actually, though, you are only staring at a piece of glass, which, as everyone knows, cannot show the world exactly as it is: everything in a mirror is reversed.

The Hallucinatory Effect comes from creating a perfect copy of an object, a place, a person. This copy acts as a kind of dummy – people take it for the real thing, because it has the physical appearance of the real thing. This is the preeminent technique of con artists, who strategically mimic the real world to deceive you. It also has applications in any arena that requires camouflage.

Image: The Shield of Perseus, polished into a reflecting mirror. Medusa cannot see you, only her own hideousness reflected back at her. Behind such a mirror you can deceive, mock, and infuriate. With one blow you sever Medusa's unsuspecting head.

Authority: The task of a military operation is to accord deceptively with the intentions of the enemy ... get to what they want first, subtly anticipate them. Maintain discipline and adapt to the enemy ... Thus, at first you are like a maiden, so the enemy opens his door; then you are like a rabbit on the loose, so the enemy cannot keep you out. (Sun-tzu, fourth century B.C.)

PREACH THE NEED
FOR CHANGE,
BUT NEVER REFORM
TOO MUCH AT ONCE

JUDGMENT

Everyone understands the need for change in the abstract, but on the day-to-day level people are creatures of habit. Too much innovation is traumatic, and will lead to revolt. If you are new to a position of power, or an outsider trying to build a power base, make a show of respecting the old way of doing things. If change is necessary, make it feel like a gentle improvement on the past.

KEYS TO POWER

Human psychology contains many dualities, one of them being that even while people understand the need for change, knowing how important it is for institutions and individuals to be occasionally renewed, they are also irritated and upset by changes that affect them personally. They know that change is necessary, and that novelty provides relief from boredom, but deep inside they cling to the past. Change in the abstract, or superficial change, they desire, but a change that upsets core habits and routines is deeply disturbing to them.

No revolution has gone without a powerful later reaction against it, for in the long run the void it creates proves too unsettling to the human animal, who unconsciously associates such voids with death and chaos. The opportunity for change and renewal seduces people to the side of the revolution, but once their enthusiasm fades, which it will, they are left with a certain emptiness. Yearning for the past, they create an opening for it to creep back in.

For Machiavelli, the prophet who preaches and brings change can only survive by taking up arms: when the masses inevitably yearn for the past, he must be ready to use force. But the armed prophet cannot last long unless he quickly creates a new set of values and rituals to replace the old ones, and to soothe the anxieties of those who dread change. It is far easier, and less bloody, to play a kind of con game. Preach change as much as you like, and even enact your reforms, but give them the comforting appearance of older events and traditions.

WHERE
CHRISTMAS
CAME FROM

Celebrating the turn of the year is an ancient custom. The Romans celebrated the Saturnalia, the festival of Saturn, god of the harvest, between December 17 and 23. It was the most cheerful festival of the year. All work and commerce stopped, and the streets were filled with crowds and a carnival atmosphere. Slaves were temporarily freed, and the houses were decorated with laurel branches. People visited one another, bringing gifts of wax candles and little clay figurines. Long before the birth of Christ, the Jews celebrated an eight-day Festival of

Lights [at the same season], and it is believed that the Germanic peoples held a great festival not only at midsummer but also at the winter solstice, when they celebrated the rebirth of the sun and honored the great fertility gods Wotan and Freyja, Donar (Thor) and Freyr ... In the year 274 the Roman Emperor Aurelian (A.D. 214–75) had established an official cult of the sun-god Mithras, declaring his birthday, December 25, a national holiday. The cult of Mithras, the Aryan god of light, had spread from Persia through Asia Minor to Greece, Rome, and as far as the Germanic lands and Britain. Numerous ruins

A simple gesture like using an old title, or keeping the same number for a group, will tie you to the past and support you with the authority of history.

Another strategy to disguise change is to make a loud and public display of support for the values of the past. Seem to be a zealot for tradition and few will notice how unconventional you really are. Renaissance Florence had a centuries-old republic, and was suspicious of anyone who flouted its traditions. Cosimo de' Medici made a show of enthusiastic support for the republic, while in reality he worked to bring the city under the control of his wealthy family. In form, the Medicis retained the appearance of a republic; in substance they rendered it powerless. They quietly enacted a radical change, while appearing to safeguard tradition.

The answer to people's innate conservatism is to play lip service to tradition. Identify the elements in your revolution that can be made to seem to build on the past. Say the right things, make a show of conformity, and meanwhile let your theories do their radical work.

Finally, powerful people pay attention to the zeitgeist. If their reform is too far ahead of its time, few will understand it, and it will stir up anxiety and be hopelessly misinterpreted. The changes you make must seem less innovative than they are.

Watch the zeitgeist. If you work in a tumultuous time, there is power to be gained by preaching a return to the past, to comfort, tradition, and ritual. During a period of stagnation, on the other hand, play the card of reform and revolution – but beware of what you stir up. Those who finish a revolution are rarely those who start it.

Image: The Cat.
Creature of habit, it loves the warmth of the familiar. Upset its routines, disrupt its space, and it will grow unmanageable and psychotic. Placate it by supporting its rituals. If change is necessary, deceive the cat by keeping the smell of the past alive; place objects familiar to it in strategic locations.

Authority: He who desires or attempts to reform the government of a state, and wishes to have it accepted, must at least retain the semblance of the old forms; so that it may seem to the people that there has been no change in the institutions, even though in fact they are entirely different from the old ones. For the great majority of mankind are satisfied with appearances, as though they were realities. (Niccolò Machiavelli, 1469–1527)

of his shrines still testify to the high regard in which this god was held, especially by the Roman legions, as a bringer of fertility, peace, and victory. So it was a clever move when, in the year A.D. 354, the Christian church under Pope Liberius (352–66) co-opted the birthday of Mithras and declared December 25 to be the birthday of Jesus Christ.

ANNE-SUSANNE RISCHKE, NEUE ZÜRCHER ZEITUNG, DECEMBER 25, 1983

NEVER APPEAR
TOO PERFECT

JUDGMENT

Appearing better than others is always dangerous, but most dangerous of all is to appear to have no faults or weaknesses. Envy creates silent enemies. It is smart to occasionally display defects, and admit to harmless vices, in order to deflect envy and appear more human and approachable. Only gods and the dead can seem perfect with impunity.

KEYS TO POWER

The human animal has a hard time dealing with feelings of inferiority. In the face of superior skill, talent, or power, we are often disturbed and ill at ease; this is because most of us have an inflated sense of ourselves, and when we meet people who surpass us they make it clear to us that we are in fact mediocre, or at least not as brilliant as we had thought. This disturbance in our self-image cannot last long without stirring up ugly emotions. At first we feel envy. But envy brings us neither comfort nor any closer to equality. Nor can we admit to feeling it, for it is frowned upon socially – to show envy is to admit to feeling inferior. So we disguise it in many ways, like finding grounds to criticize the person who makes us feel it.

There are several strategies for dealing with the insidious, destructive emotion of envy. First, understand that as you gain power, those below you will feel envious of you. They may not show it but it is inevitable. Do not naively accept the façade they show you – read between the lines of their criticisms, their little sarcastic remarks, the signs of backstabbing, the excessive praise that is preparing you for a fall, the resentful look in the eye. Half the problem with envy comes when we do not recognize it until it is too late.

Second, expect that when people envy you they will work against you insidiously. They will put obstacles in your path that you will not foresee. It is hard to defend yourself against this kind of attack. Since it is far easier to avoid creating envy in the first place than to get rid of it once it is there, you

The envious hides as carefully as the secret, lustful sinner and becomes the endless inventor of tricks and stratagems to hide and mask himself. Thus he is able to pretend to ignore the superiority of others which eats up his heart, as if he did not see them, nor hear them, nor were aware of them, nor had ever heard of them. He is a master simulator. On the other hand he tries with all his power to connive and thus prevent any form of superiority from appearing in any situation. And if they do, he casts on them obscurity, hypercriticism, sarcasm and calumny like the toad that spits poison from its hole. On the other hand he will raise

should strategize to forestall it before it grows. By becoming conscious of those actions and qualities that create envy, you can take the teeth out of it before it nibbles you to death.

A great danger in the realm of power is the sudden improvement in fortune – an unexpected promotion, a victory or success that seems to come out of nowhere. This is sure to stir up envy among your former peers.

When Archbishop Retz was promoted to the rank of cardinal, in 1651, he knew full well that many of his former colleagues envied him. Understanding the foolishness of alienating those below him, Retz did everything he could to downplay his merit and emphasize the role of luck in his success. To put people at ease, he acted humbly and deferentially, as if nothing had changed. He wrote that these wise policies "produced a good effect, by lessening the envy which was conceived against me." Follow Retz's example. Subtly emphasize how lucky you have been, to make your happiness seem more attainable to other people, and the need for envy less acute.

To deflect envy, display a weakness, a minor social indiscretion, a harmless vice.

Beware of some of envy's disguises. Excessive praise is an almost sure sign that the person praising you envies you; they are either setting you up for a fall – it will be impossible for you to live up to their praise – or they are sharpening their blades behind your back. At the same time, those who are hypercritical of you, or who slander you publicly, probably envy you as well. Recognize their behavior as disguised envy and you keep out of the trap of mutual mud-slinging, or of taking their criticisms to heart. Win your revenge by ignoring or avoiding their measly presence, leaving them to stew in a hell of their own creation.

Image: A Garden of Weeds. You may not feed them but they spread as you water the garden. You may not see how, but they take over, tall and ugly, preventing anything beautiful from flourishing. Before it is too late, do not water indiscriminately. Destroy the weeds of envy by giving them nothing to feed on.

Authority: Upon occasion, reveal a harmless defect in your character. For the envious accuse the most perfect of sinning by having no sins. They become an Argus, all eyes for finding fault with excellence – it is their only consolation. Do not let envy burst with its own venom – affect some lapse in valor or intellect, so as to disarm it beforehand. You thus wave your red cape before the Horns of Envy, in order to save your immortality. (Baltasar Gracian, 1601–1658)

For not many men, the proverb says, can love a friend who fortune prospers without feeling envy; and about the envious brain, cold poison clings and doubles all the pain life brings him. His own woundings he must nurse, and feels another's gladness like a curse.

AGAMEMNON, AESCHYLUS, C. 525–456 B.C.

It takes great talent and skill to conceal one's talent and skill.

LA ROCHEFOUCAULD, 1613–1680

DO NOT GO PAST THE
MARK YOU AIMED FOR;
IN VICTORY,
LEARN WHEN TO STOP

JUDGMENT

The moment of victory is often the moment of greatest peril. In the heat of victory, arrogance and overconfidence can push you past the goal you had aimed for, and by going too far, you make more enemies than you defeat. Do not allow success to go to your head. There is no substitute for strategy and careful planning. Set a goal, and when you reach it, stop.

KEYS TO POWER

Power has its own rhythms and patterns. Those who succeed at the game are the ones who control the patterns and vary them at will, keeping people off balance while they set the tempo. The essence of strategy is controlling what comes next, and the elation of victory can upset your ability to control what comes next in two ways. First, you owe your success to a pattern that you are apt to try to repeat. You will try to keep moving in the same direction without stopping to see whether this is still the direction that is best for you. Second, success tends to go to your head and make you emotional. Feeling invulnerable, you make aggressive moves that ultimately undo the victory you have gained.

The lesson is simple: The powerful vary their rhythms and patterns, change course, adapt to circumstance, and learn to improvise. Rather than letting their dancing feet impel them forward, they step back and look where they are going. It is as if their bloodstream bore a kind of antidote to the intoxication of victory, letting them control their emotions and come to a kind of mental halt when they have attained success. They steady themselves, give themselves the space to reflect on what has happened, examine the role of circumstance and luck in their success.

Luck and circumstance always play a role in power. But despite what you may think, good luck is more dangerous than bad luck. Bad luck teaches valuable lessons about patience, timing, and the need to be prepared for the worst; good luck deludes you

Two cockerels fought on a dungheap. One cockerel was the stronger: he vanquished the other and drove him from the dungheap. All the hens gathered around the cockerel, and began to laud him. The cockerel wanted his strength and glory to be known in the next yard. He flew on top of the barn, flapped his wings, and crowed in a loud voice: "Look at me, all of you. I am a victorious cockerel. No other cockerel in the world has such strength as I."
The cockerel had not finished, when an eagle killed him, seized him in his claws, and carried him to his nest.

FABLES, LEO
TOLSTOY,
1828–1910

into the opposite lesson, making you think your brillliance will carry you through. Your fortune will inevitably turn, and when it does you will be completely unprepared. The good luck that elevates you or seals your success brings the moment for you to open your eyes: the wheel of fortune will hurtle you down as easily as up. If you prepare for the fall, it is less likely to ruin you when it happens.

The rhythm of power often requires an alternation of force and cunning. Too much force creates a counterreaction; too much cunning, no matter how cunning it is, becomes predictable. When you are victorious, then, lay low, and lull the enemy into inaction. These changes of rhythm are immensely powerful.

People who go past the mark are often motivated by a desire to please a master by proving their dedication. But an excess of effort exposes you to the risk of making the master suspicious of you. On several occasions, generals under Philip of Macedon were disgraced and demoted immediately after leading their troops to a great victory; one more such victory, Philip thought, and the man might become a rival instead of an underling. When you serve a master, it is often wise to measure your victories carefully, letting him get the glory and never making him uneasy. It is also wise to establish a pattern of strict obedience to earn his trust.

Finally, the moment when you stop has great dramatic import. What comes last sticks in the mind as a kind of exclamation point. There is no better time to stop and walk away than after a victory. Keep going and you risk lessening the effect, even ending up defeated. As lawyers say of cross-examination, "Always stop with a victory."

> Image: Icarus Falling from the Sky. His father Daedalus fashions wings of wax that allow the two men to fly out of the labyrinth and escape the Minotaur. Elated by the triumphant escape and the feeling of flight, Icarus soars higher and higher, until the sun melts the wings and he hurtles to his death.

Authority: Princes and republics should content themselves with victory, for when they aim at more, they generally lose. The use of insulting language toward an enemy arises from the insolence of victory, or from the false hope of victory, which latter misleads men as often in their actions as in their words; for when this false hope takes possession of the mind, it makes men go beyond the mark, and causes them to sacrifice a certain good for an uncertain better. (Niccolò Machiavelli, 1469–1527)

ASSUME FORMLESSNESS

JUDGMENT

By taking a shape, by having a visible plan, you open yourself to attack. Instead of taking a form for your enemy to grasp, keep yourself adaptable and on the move. Accept the fact that nothing is certain and no law is fixed. The best way to protect yourself is to be as fluid and formless as water; never bet on stability or lasting order. Everything changes.

KEYS TO POWER

The human animal is distinguished by its constant creation of forms. Rarely expressing its emotions directly, it gives them form through language, or through socially acceptable rituals. We cannot communicate our emotions without a form.

The forms that we create, however, change constantly – in fashion, in style, in all those human phenomena representing the mood of the moment. We are constantly altering the forms we have inherited from previous generations, and these changes are signs of life and vitality. Indeed the things that don't change, the forms that rigidify, come to look to us like death, and we destroy them.

The powerful are often people who in their youth have shown immense creativity in expressing something new through a new form. Society grants them power because it hungers for and rewards this sort of newness. The problem comes later, when they often grow conservative and possessive. They no longer dream of creating new forms; their identities are set, their habits congeal, and their rigidity makes them easy targets.

Power can only thrive if it is flexible in its forms. To be formless is not to be amorphous; everything has a form – it is impossible to avoid. The formlessness of power is more like that of water, or mercury, taking the form of whatever is around it. Changing constantly, it is never predictable.

The first psychological requirement of formlessness is to train yourself to take nothing personally. Never show any defensiveness. When you act defensive, you show your emotions, revealing a clear form. Your

In martial arts, it is important that strategy be unfathomable, that form be concealed, and that movements be unexpected, so that preparedness against them be impossible. What enables a good general to win without fail is always having unfathomable wisdom and a modus operandi that leaves no tracks. Only the formless cannot be affected. Sages hide in unfathomability, so their feelings cannot be observed; they operate in formlessness, so their lines cannot be crossed.

THE BOOK OF
THE HUAINAN
MASTERS, CHINA,
SECOND CENTURY
B.C.

The sage neither seeks to follow the ways of the ancients nor establishes any fixed standard for all times but examines the things of his age and then prepares to deal with them. There was in Sung a man, who tilled a field in which there stood the trunk of a tree. Once a hare, while running fast, rushed against the trunk, broke its neck, and died. Thereupon the man cast his plough aside and watched that tree, hoping that he would get another hare. Yet he never caught another hare and was himself ridiculed by the people of Sung. Now supposing somebody wanted to govern the people of the present age with the policies of the early kings, he would

opponents will realize they have hit a nerve, an Achilles' heel. And they will hit it again and again. Make your face a formless mask and you will infuriate and disorient your scheming colleagues and opponents.

One man who used this technique was Baron James Rothschild. A German Jew in Paris, in a culture decidedly unfriendly to foreigners, Rothschild never took any attack on him personally. He furthermore adapted himself to the political climate, whatever it was. Rothschild accepted them one and all, and blended in. While he adapted and thrived, never showing a form, all the other great families that had begun the century immensely wealthy were ruined in the period's complicated shifts and turns of fortune. Attaching themselves to the past, they revealed their embrace of a form.

As you get older, you must rely even less on the past. Be vigilant lest the form your character has taken makes you seem a relic.

Never forget, though, that formlessness is a strategic pose. It gives you room to create tactical surprises; as your enemies struggle to guess your next move, they reveal their own strategy, putting them at a decided disadvantage. It keeps the initiative on your side, putting your enemies in the position of never acting, constantly reacting. It foils their spying and intelligence. Remember: Formlessness is a tool. Never confuse it with a go-with-the-flow style, or with a religious resignation to the twists of fortune. You use formlessness, not because it creates inner harmony and peace, but because it will increase your power.

Finally, learning to adapt to each new

circumstance means seeing events through your own eyes, and often ignoring the advice that people constantly peddle your way. It means that ultimately you must throw out the laws that others preach, and the books they write to tell you what to do, and the sage advice of the elder. Rely too much on other people's ideas and you end up taking a form not of your own making. Be brutal with the past, especially your own, and have no respect for the philosophies that are foisted on you from outside.

be doing exactly the same thing as that man who watched the tree.

HAN-FEI-TZU, CHINESE PHILOSOPHER, THIRD CENTURY B.C.

Image: Mercury. The winged messenger, god of commerce, patron saint of thieves, gamblers, and all those who deceive through swiftness. The day Mercury was born, he invented the lyre; by that evening he had stolen the cattle of Apollo. He would scour the world, assuming whatever form he desired. Like the liquid metal named after him, he embodies the elusive, the ungraspable – the power of formlessness.

Authority: Therefore the consummation of forming an army is to arrive at formlessness. Victory in war is not repetitious, but adapts its form endlessly … A military force has no constant formation, water has no constant shape: the ability to gain victory by changing and adapting according to the opponent is called genius. (Sun-Tzu, fourth century B.C.)